AF445272

UNSEEN FORCES

UNSEEN FORCES

A SEARCH FOR THE SACRED
IN A DARKENED WORLD

by Roy Whitten

Unseen Forces Press

Dedication

For Jeanne, as always

CONTENTS

PROLOGUE

THE RIGHT QUESTIONS

*A national rupture demonstrates the need for
sacred understanding
Three fundamental questions drive the search*

On January 6, 2021, I watched a live broadcast from Washington, D.C. On the television screen above the cabinet in my study, a white man with a gray beard drove a riot shield into a first-floor window of the U.S. Capitol. The glass shattered, the window frame collapsed, and a woman lifted a smartphone to record the moment. People dressed in camouflage, red hats, and backpacks broke into the very building whose ideals they claimed to defend.

I hated to watch, but I couldn't look away.

The crest of this wave had been building for decades. In 1979, I went public with my theological concerns about Jerry Falwell and his Moral Majority: a theocratic political movement that sought to impose Fundamentalist beliefs and ethics on all Americans. I shared my concerns with my small, Episcopal congregation, and one of my sermons led to a lecture for the National Conference of Christians and Jews. Other organizations asked me to speak, and Owen Spann invited me three times to be a guest on his KGO Radio talk show in San Francisco. The pushback from local Fundamentalists and my own church was organized, personal, and threatening. I had a family to raise and a living to earn.

My concern mushroomed into fear. I quit speaking publicly, and I stood on the sidelines as the movement now called Christian Nationalism slowly gathered force.

Forty years later, the tragedy on my television screen seemed an inevitable development. In the name of democracy—a form of governance founded on the notion of equality and rationality—violence had now become an acceptable form of protest. Moreover, according to the theology driving the protest, the violence was sanctioned by God.

I had enough common sense to recognize unChristian behavior when I saw it and enough theological training to understand the fundamentalist flaws that drove it. In his essay, "Equality," C.S. Lewis expressed the theological wisdom underlying the framing of the American Constitution: "Mankind is so fallen that no man can be trusted with unchecked power over his fellows." Given people's tendency to create a God that allows them to pursue their own fear-driven ends, the separation of church and state is an essential safeguard to American democracy. The Capitol riot was a painful demonstration of the power of religious passion to steamroll basic human decency.

I wanted to do something to help, but what? Four decades ago, I was young and frightened of public pushback. Now, with plenty of success and failure under my belt, fear had given way to an anxiety refreshed daily by the latest headlines, and I was not alone: my anxiety was shared by many across the spectrum of religion and politics.

But there was something about my growing concern I didn't trust. I felt myself taking sides, judging the rioters I watched, especially those brandishing Christian symbols and waving signs proclaiming, "*God* chose Trump." *What's wrong with them? How can they think this is what God wants them to do? Who or what do they actually worship?*

Theologian and political commentator, Reinhold Niebuhr, once warned: "There are no right answers to the wrong questions." I was a 73-year-old priest with three careers under my belt, two of them outside religious circles. Along the way, I'd asked plenty of wrong questions and, given my leadership responsibilities, I wasn't the only one who had suffered the consequences. I was worried: for myself, for the people I love, and for the future of my country. To do something constructive about my concerns, I needed more effective questions, questions that examined my own convictions *before* I addressed the convictions of others.

A phrase came to mind, something I read fifty years ago in a book by Professor Jacob Needleman of San Francisco State University. I'd never been able to find his exact words, but this was my memory of what he wrote: "Our lives are shaped by unseen forces that we'll never fully understand, but which we can learn to serve." "Unseen forces" aptly described what unfolded on my television screen, *and* what I felt in my gut.

At that moment in 2021, I had retired from the business I co-founded and decided that I would spend my remaining years writing more books. I had enrolled in an MFA program to sharpen my skills, and I intended to write about the forces that influenced who I am, what I believe, and what I do. I started my search with one "right" question: What happened to me, wondrous and tragic, that shaped my life?

To answer this question, I had to return to childhood and follow a journey that seemed to have three distinct passages, each with its stumbles and breakthroughs, missed opportunities and moments of transcendence. I had to learn some hard truths: faith is action, not belief; beliefs must be grounded in experience; beliefs can be wrong, even when they feel right; and humility is required to update belief when experience demands it. I had to confront the power of my mind: its capacity to create understanding *and* self-deception. I had to resist its ability to drive my darker impulses by generating fear about things beyond my control, and I had to cultivate its capacity for self-awareness and discovery. I had to admit what I *really* believed: about life, about death, about life after death, and about who or what ultimately to trust. I had to accept that what I really believed about "God" was perfectly reflected in what I did with my time, my money, my vote, and my deepest desires for the world in which I live and will pass on to my children and grandchildren.

I also had to learn how to talk with others about things that drove us apart instead of bringing us together, those topics of conversation best avoided at family gatherings: politics, religion, and what we ultimately believe and why. I had to learn how to stand on my own convictions and respect the convictions of others without falling into the trap of mistaking passion for fact, imagination for reality, or fervent certainty for actual understanding.

This is the story of my own search for the sacred in the twists and turns of my life. I intend it to generate conversation, not debate. Whenever possible, I refer to people by name. I'm closing in on 80, and a lot of these people have died. I want to honor the role they played in my life. I know my comments about others are my perceptions and not the truth. In the few places where identifying someone might be hurtful, I openly invent a name.

The January insurrection was tragic and dramatic, but it wasn't unprecedented, and as we've seen, it wasn't the last event of its kind. Finding and answering the "right" questions about the unseen forces is a struggle, but this struggle shows me the way to serve the best of these forces and make a constructive contribution to our common future.

Roy Whitten

December, 2025

PASSAGE I

WONDER, CERTAINTY, AND CORRECTION

1954-1971 — AGE 7-24

My search begins with a few experiences I can't understand but which shaped my life.

Chapter 1

Unexplained Wonders

Age 7-12
Extraordinary things happen
Outside myself and inside
They don't make sense, and nobody explains them

THE TREE

Until the middle of my tenth year, I lived in the dusty, Southern California town of Camarillo. It had one main street, one school for children from kindergarten through eighth grade, and one movie theater. It was a safe environment; at seven years of age, I regularly rode my bike four blocks to the town's theater, left the bike unlocked while I watched a double-feature, and hours later rode it back home.

Our backyard butted up against a bean field. I remember an afternoon when I crossed the patio and threaded my way through the razor-sharp pampas grass that Dad had planted to keep animals off our property. I followed the edge of the bean field as it climbed the gentle hill that bordered the yards of our neighbors. The field was newly plowed, and I raised clouds of dust as I crushed the peak of every row I crossed. The Santa Ana wind blew hot and dry. Sweat caked on my face and tasted of salt. I reached the top of the hill adjacent to the highest point of

5

Grandview Circle, the road my best friend, Jimmy, and I lived on.

I walked downhill past the last of the houses and into a quarry that, years before, had produced the gravel and sand used to make the building foundations, sidewalks, and patios of our town. There were still mounds of large and small rocks in the abandoned quarry, and Jimmy and I had often climbed the piles and aimed the rocks at trees, bushes, and stray animals. This day, however, I felt drawn to a grove of tall fir trees that somehow survived all the digging. I chose the tallest tree in the grove and started to climb.

The branches were scratchy, but soft: not like pine needles that drew blood, but gentle on the skin. They smelled like Christmas. I tilted my head forward to protect my eyes and pushed my head and shoulders through the boughs. Halfway up, I felt the tree moving in the wind, and the branches grew closer together. I nestled into them, and they closed around me. I climbed as high as I dared and looked out. Camarillo was spread out below. The Santa Ana wind pushed the tree from side-to-side. I swallowed hard, and wrapped my arms around the trunk, squeezed it between my knees, and closed my eyes.

I swayed in the breeze, and a warmth rose from the bottom of my stomach to the top of my head. I knew I belonged here. I wanted to tell Mom and Dad, but I was afraid they'd think I didn't like being at home.

That night, I didn't say much at dinner. The stillness stayed with me.

TWO STICKS

Unless Mom or Dad insisted, I never invited my little brother to play with Jimmy and me. John couldn't keep up, he kept knocking the toy soldiers over instead of setting them in rows, and he couldn't catch a football or ride a bike fast. And, when I didn't let him play with me, he caused trouble.

One day, I became a "cowboy." I straddled a sawhorse and lassoed the shovel handle that stuck out of a wheelbarrow full of dirt Dad used to plant the garden.

"*I* want to be a cowboy."

It was John, of course, who for a while had been content to stand by the wheelbarrow and watch. "Please," he said. When I didn't answer, he narrowed his eyes and lowered his voice. "If you don't let me play, I'll tell Mom, and you'll get it."

I ignored him, and threw the lasso at the shovel. John picked up the rope, held it, and looked right at me. I jerked the line. Once. Twice. I'd pull him over if he didn't let go. He put the rope between his teeth and smiled.

We both knew if anything happened to his teeth, all hell would break loose.

You little bastard. Fine. If that's the way you want it, you can have it. I yanked on the rope. He opened his eyes wide and covered his mouth with both hands. Blood gushed out between his fingers. He started screaming. Everyone came running. He stood there, blood running down his arms, waiting for Mom and Dad to feel sorry for him, take care of him, and punish me for hurting him. That, of course, is exactly what happened.

A couple of weeks later, both of us went to summer camp. It wasn't really a camp, but a week of activities at our church that gave kids something to do and gave parents a breather. During the first two days of camp, I did all I could to avoid being with John. I was still pissed off about the rope. On Wednesday, Mom announced John had a stomachache. He had a lot of stomach-aches. I was delighted to go to camp by myself.

"I'll bring him later if he feels better," Mom said. I hoped he felt miserable all day long.

That day, camp was great. No little brother underfoot. No one to look out for, drag along, explain things to, or help with one thing or another. And it was kite day! The classroom tables were stocked with kite-making supplies: sticks of wood with notches on each end, balls of string, newspapers, colored cloth, rulers, dowel rods, scissors, and glue.

"I'm going to show you how to make a kite from scratch," said Sam, the overly enthusiastic teenager who led our group. During the next hour, I tied a long stick to a shorter one and made a cross. "You've got to make the kite as light as possible," Sam said, "so it can fly high." I stretched string around the frame, threaded it carefully through the notches at the ends of the sticks. I placed the stringed frame on a full sheet of newspaper and carefully cut the paper around the frame. I left a one-inch border, folded the paper over the string, and glued it into place.

While the glue dried, I cut pieces of cloth, one inch wide, six inches long, and tied them ten inches apart to the bottom of the kite. I took a new ball of string, tied it to the center of the kite, and wound the string around a thick dowel rod. After a snack break, we all took our kites to the field for a test run.

The Santa Ana was perfect for flying kites, but something wasn't right with mine. Instead of rising steadily as I let out line, it snapped left and right, falling several feet before shooting up again.

"You need a longer tail," said Sam. "I'll reel it in while you cut some more cloth."

I raced back to the classroom to make another two feet of tail. I opened the door and saw John. Mom had brought him late, and he'd found his way to the room. He stood at a table, two thin sticks of wood in his little hands, eyes scrunched up, tears running down his cheeks. He didn't move; he just looked at me and whimpered.

My eyes got wet, and my throat tightened. Here was this confused little boy whose stomach ached in the morning, who couldn't keep up with his big brother, alone and crying because he didn't know what to do with those two sticks.

I don't know how much time it took, but I helped him build a kite. I even let him do the easy parts. He managed to tie the sticks into a cross. I guided the string through the notches and cut paper to go around the frame. John laid the line of glue, wrapped the paper around the string, and picked out the material for the tail.

I took him to the field and showed him how to reel out string from the dowel rod as I walked twenty steps away, letting the Santa Ana push me. As I raised the kite into the air, and watched it take off like a rocket, he stared with his mouth open. And then he laughed out loud.

I didn't remember to lengthen the tail on my own kite. It didn't matter, because I spent the rest of the day with my brother, flying his.

THE BIKE

Three years later, we moved 300 miles north to San Jose. One Saturday afternoon, I rode my bike to a small shopping center a mile from home. I bought a few things—a new record, a baseball, folders and pencils for school— and strapped them to the carrier over my back wheel. When I got home, the box of pencils was missing. I didn't have time to ride back to the shopping center, and I hit on the idea of taking the trip in my mind. I sat in the front yard, closed my eyes, and recalled the moment I came out of the store and clamped my purchases to the carrier. A peacefulness came over me as, block-by-block and turn-by-turn, I replayed the ride home. My brake chain was loose, and I stopped in front of a blue house, up the block from where we lived, I got off my bike, adjusted the chain, and when I took off, I heard something hit the sidewalk behind me.

I opened my eyes, got on my bike, and rode to the blue house. There, on the sidewalk, was the box of pencils. As I rode home, I wondered what else my mind could do.

THE DESIRE

I remember a teacher named Mr. Orser who visited our home in the summer of 1957. He asked me to sit with him and my parents while he explained the logistics of an experimental sixth grade program he would conduct when school started in the fall. He was a thin, owlish man who somehow obtained permission to try something new with over-achieving kids and supportive parents.

He sat on our living room couch, and talked not just to Mom and Dad, but also to me. I sat up straighter as he described what I'd be doing.

"My plan," he explained, "is to have you, Roy, tackle the entire sixth-grade curriculum *after* school: the reading, the exercises, the regular classwork. It's a lot of homework, but it frees you to spend the entire school day doing research, writing reports, and sharing what you learn with your classmates."

"Reports?" I was suspicious. "On what?"

"Whatever you want to learn more about." He beamed as he said this.

"Anything?"

"Anything."

Mom turned to me and said, "Are you sure you want to do this?"

I felt my chest get larger. "You bet."

Mr. Orser stuck to his plan. Encyclopedias, art supplies,

records, and musical instruments lined the classroom. My first report was on the history of baseball, the second on the history of football, the third on the history of basketball. For some reason lost in time, I wrote my fourth report on the Alaskan Tundra. That year, I toured the world in my imagination, learned to dance the Bop, and studied like crazy every day after school. I came home from school, had a snack, did homework until dinner, and then more homework until bedtime. Mom later said she'd never seen me work so hard.

During one of those long weekday evenings, finishing the sixth-grade curriculum for the day, I decided I needed to read more. I remember thinking, *Books are windows to the world.* I must have read that sentence somewhere, and I knew it was true. With this thought came a plan: start by reading what I *want* to read.

The following Saturday, I rode to the Cupertino library, a half mile from our home. I spent an hour looking through the stacks. It all looked pretty boring. Then, I wandered into the biography section and found stories about athletes. I checked out seven books: biographies of Willie Mays, Mickey Mantle, Lou Gehrig, a couple of football and basketball players, and the building of The Green Monster: the huge left-field wall at Boston's Fenway Park.

On Saturday mornings, for months thereafter, I pedaled to the library, returned the books I'd read the week before, and chose seven new ones. I only borrowed the books I wanted, and I figured my wants would change over time, just like they had in Mr. Orser's class. By the end of the year, I was exploring most of the library's shelves.

Evidently, I had the ability to change myself.

THE FUTURE

I was twelve, and near the end of the final game of my last year in Little League baseball. It had been a miserable season. Either we got slaughtered from the start, or we held on for a few innings and then we got slaughtered. We just couldn't win.

On this day, however, a miracle was in the making. It was the bottom of the fifth inning, and we'd just scored four runs. We were bouncing around the dugout like caged monkeys, slapping each other on the back, beginning to believe this just might be it: our only win of the season. When Bobby grounded out, ending our turn at bat, the coach gathered us together. He was a kindly man who months ago had given up on winning and repeatedly encouraged us to "just have some fun." Now, however, his eyes were wide and his face serious.

"Okay, boys. All we have to do is keep them from scoring twice. Get out there and do it!"

We raced onto the field, yelling encouragement to each other. The infield dirt crunched beneath my shoes, and I smelled cut grass as I ran to my position. Left field was where I belonged; I didn't have a strong enough arm for center, but I was fast and covered a lot of ground. Thank God, I wasn't stuck in right field, the designated spot for the weakest player on the team. I took my position in the outfield grass; I crouched, hands on my knees, eyes on our pitcher.

Their first batter got a single, a solid shot over the shortstop's head. I fielded it cleanly and threw it to second base to hold the runner at first. The next batter struck out, and I felt my heart beat faster. The next player laid down a perfect sacrifice bunt and advanced the runner to second. I took a deep breath. There was one out. Even if they managed to bring the runner home, we'd still be ahead by a run, and the game would be ours.

"We can do this!" I yelled. As their next batter approached the plate, the players in our dugout shook the chain-link fence and started the chant: "Hey batter batter, hey, batter batter." Our pitcher threw three straight strikes, and now there were two outs. God, this was it. One more out.

The fourth batter hit it hard and high, soaring in my direction. I froze for a moment, unsure how far the ball would fly. It climbed higher, and I sprinted toward the fence. I heard my shoes scrape the warning track and I stopped before I hit the wall. I watched the ball arc overhead like a rainbow headed for a pot of gold. I turned around, saw the runner round third, saw the batter punch the air with his fist, and watched their team pour out of the dugout to celebrate the tying run.

Their next player fouled out to the first baseman and ended the inning, but the damage was done. I dragged myself off the field. Sure, the game was tied, and we had the bottom of the sixth to get a run and win. But that wasn't going to happen. We were cursed. It might take one inning, it might take three, but we were going to lose, again.

Our first batter struck out. I shivered and couldn't feel my legs. Our second batter was at the plate, and I sat on the bench, kicking a Juicy Fruit gum wrapper with my cleats. The coach yelled at me: "You're on deck. Get with it."

I snapped awake, embarrassed I'd lost track of where I was supposed to be. I grabbed my bat from the rack and walked to the on-deck circle; I got there in time to watch my teammate ground out to the shortstop. Now, it was my turn to screw up. I would be the final out, that would lead to extra innings, and we'd lose our last game of the season. My legs shook as I walked to the batter's box, and I saw the catcher smile. I'd struck out my last two times at bat, and he shouted, "Easy out!"

That hurt.

I started my routine. I'd read every batter needed a routine, and I'd developed one. I tapped the outside edge of home plate with the bat, one more tap to the center of the plate, set my feet parallel to each other, pulled the bat back, raised my right elbow, and tried to ignore my legs.

The pitcher started his windup, and I heard a rushing wind. I felt rooted to the ground, my stomach was warm and relaxed, I felt the grain of the wood on my bat, and then everything … stopped. A soft light filled the field, and I watched a scene unfold.

The pitcher throws the ball. I swing late and hit it off the end of the bat. The twisty grounder skips between the legs of the first baseman and spins away from the right fielder. I round first base and make it to second. The third base coach flashes the "steal" sign, and on the next pitch, I slide into third just ahead of the tag. The pitcher throws the next pitch over the catcher's head, and I race home with the winning run.

The scene ended, I snapped awake: in the batter's box, holding the bat, the pitcher bringing his arm forward. The ball headed for the center of the plate, and everything played out just as I'd seen it in that flash of a second. I swung late, the first baseman missed the ball, I made it to second, stole third, and I slid safely home on a wild pitch. My teammates lifted me from the ground and pounded me on the back. They must have been cheering, but all I heard was the rasp of my breath.

For the next few hours, I was two people: one whooped it up while the other tried to figure out what the hell had just happened. Over a celebratory ice cream, I tried to tell my family I'd seen the future, but Dad only smiled and said, "I'm sure you did." He seemed nervous, changed the subject, and didn't mention it again.

I forgot about it, for years.

SOMETHING SPECIAL

I'm intrigued. There's a lot more to me than I know. Some impulse asserts itself. I can't deny what happened: the sense of a deeper self, an eruption of genuine care, the ability to recover memory, the power of my desire, and the ability to glimpse the future. But I can't explain any of it. The people around me don't believe it happened, and I learn to keep it to myself.

There's something special about who I am and what I can do.

Chapter 2

TOO SURE FOR MY OWN GOOD

Age 12-19
Childhood provided questions I couldn't answer
Adolescence brings answers I don't question
Not every instinct is sound, not every lesson is learned

SURE ABOUT EXCELLING

My liberating sixth grade experience with Mr. Orser was followed by two years I often describe as the worst in my life. At Elvira Castro Jr. High School, students fought at least once a week, occasionally with knives. Shop teachers paddled kids for minor infractions, and, with devastating accuracy, my math instructor threw blackboard chalk at anyone who didn't pay attention.

My seventh grade English teacher was an irritable man whose last name started with "B" and ended in "ian." I remember him as "Mr. Bukajian," although that most certainly wasn't his name. I'd learned from Mr. Orser the way to be a good student was to follow my interests and share what I found. I did that freely in Mr. Bukajian's class, and I expected the praise I'd received before. The school year was divided into three "quarters" (the fourth quarter being summer vacation), and on a Friday, at the end of the first quarter, he distributed our report cards. He had given me a "C."

It was the lowest grade I'd ever received, and after school, when I presented the card to my mother, I broke into tears.

The following Monday morning, at the start of that class, the speaker mounted in the upper corner of the classroom beeped loudly, signaling a message from the administration. "Roy Whitten, pick up all your belongings and report to the principal's office."

Mr. Bukajian glared at me and snapped, "Get out of here." Humiliated, I did what I was told and left the room. Without explanation, the principal assigned me to a different class.

When I told my parents what had happened, my mother uttered one word: "Good."

I asked what she meant.

"When you showed me your report card last week, I drove to your school and caught your teacher before he left for the day. I told him I was concerned about you—that you were not a C-student, and what could I do to help. He said, 'I'm sick and tired of Orser's smart-aleck kids. Your son got a "C" this quarter, he'll get a "D" next quarter, and an "F" after that.'"

My stomach dropped. *An "F!" I'm going to flunk seventh grade!*

Mom continued: "I looked him right in the eye and said, 'Come Monday morning, my son won't be in your class.'"

So that's why I was transferred.

I took a deep breath. That jerk, Bukajian, was punishing me for being intelligent, and "Mommy" had to rescue me. I spent the rest of the afternoon in my room, stoking my rage and ignoring my embarrassment.

SURE ABOUT ACTING

In my final year at Blackford High School, nearly two hundred faculty and students spent four months preparing to stage the school's first-ever musical: *My Fair Lady*. The drama club provided the cast, the music department fielded the orchestra, the wood and metal shops created the sets, Home Economics sewed the costumes, the art department designed posters and tickets, and the English classes handled advertising. The principal scheduled a three-night run for the middle of May.

At the first drama club meeting of the new year, Mrs. Hardy, our director, announced with fanfare she had already cast two great singers for the roles of Eliza and Freddy. Tryouts for the remaining parts, including Henry Higgins, the male lead, would take place the following Friday.

By now, I had appeared in two plays sponsored by a community organization. I discovered I liked being on stage. My shyness disappeared when I portrayed someone else, and I enjoyed playing to the audience, earning a burst of laughter or a round of applause. The movie, starring Rex Harrison and Audrey Hepburn, had just been released, and I bought a ticket. In the opening scene, Harrison stepped from behind a marble column and started to sing the song that asked the question, "Why can't the English teach their children how to speak?" I knew I was destined to play Henry Higgins.

When the movie ended, I drove across the street to Tower Records and purchased the soundtrack. By Sunday evening, I memorized every one of Higgins' songs, and three days later, I knew all his lines. At Friday's tryout, however, I didn't get a chance to perform. Mrs. Hardy had given the male lead to our English foreign exchange student.

It soon became obvious that although he sounded the part, he couldn't act, sing, or dance. For the next two weeks, I moped, fumed, and turned into a complete asshole. I belittled the poor guy behind his back and to his face. At the end of our fifth rehearsal,

I sat by myself and muttered out loud about the unfairness of it all. Mrs. Hardy yelled at me from across the room: "Are you not going to be satisfied with any part but the lead?" My face burned and I clenched my teeth. I stared at my shoelaces and thought, *You're goddamned right I won't!*

Two days later, the exchange student quit, and Mrs. Hardy gave me the role. It never occurred to me to feel guilty.

The play was a great success, and the role fit me like a glove. In the final scene, when I put on the herringbone fedora, stood alone in front of the curtain, and sang, "I've Grown Accustomed to Her Face," I *became* Henry Higgins.

On the final night of the run, Dick Taylor, a former Blackford student, attended the performance. He had graduated three years earlier, starred in several plays, was president of his class, and was now in his third year of study at the Pasadena Playhouse. The next day, he treated me to dinner and a play, told me I had what it took to be an actor, and invited me to join him in Pasadena after graduation.

My body felt free and light. This had to be the right direction for me to take.

That evening, I announced the plan to my parents. They didn't object, but I could tell they weren't thrilled. Three days later, the principal invited me to his office.

"Well," he began, "you've had a real success with *My Fair Lady.*"

"Thank you," I said, showing a humility that was improving with use.

"And you're going to attend Pasadena Playhouse in the fall?"

My mind started to race. *How does he know what I'm planning to do?*

He pressed his palms together as if in prayer. "I've been thinking about your future."

Wow. He must really like me.

"And with your intelligence and ability, I figure you can do anything you put your mind to."

Well, that's true.

"I've only got one concern."

Uh, oh.

"I'm worried your success as Henry Higgins might have been a case of typecasting."

I stopped breathing and a burning sensation crawled up my throat. Everybody in drama club knew about typecasting; you succeeded in a role not because you could act, but because the part matched your personality.

"Of course, that may not be the case here," he said. "Dick Taylor certainly thought the world of your performance." He paused for a moment. "But he's still a student; he's not an industry professional or anything like it."

I felt sweat run down my back.

The principal continued, smooth and soothing. "I have an idea you might want to consider."

Yes, please.

"You've already been accepted into San Jose State's new two-year program: Tutorials in Letters and Science. It's based on the Great Books of the Western World. You're a smart guy, and it's possible this experiment won't be repeated. The college has a good drama program. Why not take acting classes on the side, get your AA degree, and, if you still want to act for a living, go to Pasadena two years from now when you're sure of yourself?"

I left his office in a daze, but by the time I returned to class, I suspected he was right. I loved the attention, but could I really act? I wasn't Dick Taylor and didn't particularly want to be. After school, I told my parents I'd changed my mind and would attend San Jose State in the fall. They didn't seem surprised by the news, and they complimented me on the wisdom of my decision.

Two years later, I learned Mom had intervened again. After my announcement about going to Pasadena, she had marched into Principal Romer's office and demanded he fix the problem he'd caused. And that's what he did.

I worried Mom had thwarted my destiny, but I worried even more about how quickly my sense of certainty disappeared in the face of flattery and fear.

SURE ABOUT RELIGION

In the spring of 1967, I neared the completion of my sophomore year at San Jose State. I loved their Tutorials program, hated the drama classes, and decided on a double major of Philosophy and Psychology. One afternoon, I strolled through the college quad with a tall, athletic senior. I don't remember his name, where we met, or how we came to be crossing the grassy mall of the campus. I do recall how completely certain he was about what had happened to him that morning. He said, "Today, I am really walking in the Spirit!"

Walking in the Spirit. That got my attention. In fact, it got under my attention; it burrowed deep and tapped into a well of longing. He led an organization I'd never heard of called Campus Crusade for Christ. Although the words, "Crusade for Christ," set off faint Episcopalian alarm bells, his sincerity and complete trust in his own convictions overshadowed my caution.

Christianity was my spiritual north star, but my understanding of this path had been framed by ten years of belonging to the Episcopal Church. I'd listened to a lot of Scripture but never studied it. I didn't know what Christians were supposed to do, or say, or believe. My church provided the freedom to figure all that out for myself within the wide, general boundaries of common sense, decent behavior, and good taste. It emphasized serving others, especially those who had less. It valued the sense of community, of breaking bread together on Sunday mornings. It affirmed equality and justice for all, provided this stance didn't veer into any radical behavior.

At every family dinner, we'd hold hands and say grace: *Jesus, be our holy guest. Our morning joy, and our evening rest. And with thy daily bread impart thy peace and joy to every heart. Dear God, please bless this food, our friends, and our family.* I don't recall ever discussing the prayer, but at its end, Mom could be counted on to take a deep breath and occasionally remark about how peaceful the words made her feel. On Saturday evenings, Dad polished everyone's shoes, so we'd look our best for church. When our family knelt side-by-side at the communion rail, I was sure other families envied us.

Compared to what this Campus Crusade for Christ guy was talking about—*Walking in the Spirit*—my upbringing seemed polite, uncontroversial, and ineffective. He quoted extensively from the Bible, and he talked about how God guided his steps and told him what to say in difficult situations. His words were electric, tangible, and compelling. He *knew* what it meant to be a Christian.

As he spoke, I felt again the "sway" at the top of that tree in Camarillo, and I didn't think twice about accepting his invitation to a CCC meeting. Two days later, I sat in a room at a local church while he led a group of ten students on a cruise through Scripture. I marveled at his facility with the Bible. He spoke fluidly and without notes as he quoted from both the Old and New Testaments. He was impressive, and in his presence, my sense of inadequacy descended like a dark mist.

I couldn't handle feeling small. I set my doubts aside, shifted into learning mode, and attended his meetings. I quickly deduced there were five key points I was to live by, and when ready, share with others: 1) God has a plan for your life; 2) for reasons that go back to Adam and Eve and over which you have no control, you're separated from Him; 3) Jesus put an end to this separation by dying on the cross, and you can benefit from his sacrifice by accepting him into your heart as your personal Lord and Savior; 4) when you do so, God will rescue you from sin and reward your faithfulness in this life and the next; and 5) you need to get going on this because Jesus is returning soon, and God will reward the believers with heaven and punish unbelievers with hell.

Ironically, my study of the classics had trained me to set aside my own convictions to better appreciate other points of view, and this perspective had an incontestable logic. I really wanted to "Walk in the Spirit" as everyone else seemed to be doing. To a person, the rest of the group felt Christ "growing" in them, and they were over the moon about it. I couldn't generate enough cynicism to deny what they were feeling, and I ached to be as certain as they were.

I was a quick study, and soon I had the five-point plan for salvation firmly in my grasp. I could draw the diagrams to illustrate separation from God, the sacrifice of Jesus, and the union with him through faith. I memorized the key questions to ask, especially the closing one. Just when I was feeling adept, if not completely comfortable, my new friend, the leader, said, "You've made wonderful progress! I think you're ready to come with us this afternoon and offer your witness to the occupants of that green apartment on 4th Street. We're going to win the entire building for Christ!"

I didn't hesitate. It was like going on stage for *My Fair Lady*. I knew the lines and was ready to hit my marks. I too was going to "Walk in the Spirit."

Fifteen minutes later, I climbed the black metal stairs to the second floor of the lime-green apartment building on 4th Street. I knocked on the first door I found and when a student answered, I delivered my opening lines: "My friends and I are in the neighborhood today, talking with people about what happens when we die. Do you have a few minutes to discuss this with me?" I was surprised he invited me in. Obviously, God wanted us to have this conversation.

He had dark hair, cut very short, and he hadn't shaved that morning. He wore a green tee shirt, white shorts, and no shoes. He carried himself like an athlete, but he had a soft face and a gentle voice. My skin tingled, but I knew how to handle stage fright. I sat at his kitchen table and pressed onward with the Bible quotes and personal stories I'd practiced at the CCC meetings. He listened more than he talked. That was fine, because I had a lot to say. After a while, he fidgeted in his chair and stared at the black-and-white clock above where we sat. I was shocked to see I'd been talking nonstop for 45 minutes. I was losing my audience, so I went for the close.

"Well," I said, "are you ready to receive Jesus Christ as your personal Lord and Savior?"

He uncrossed his legs, put both hands on the table, and looked me right in the eye. In a clear, sardonic voice, he said, "I don't think I'll be doing that today." He stood up, waited for me to rise, escorted me to his front door, and stood aside as I slunk out. I heard the door slam behind me. I felt paint peeling into my palm as I grabbed the handrail on my way down the stairs. I looked at the pavement below and felt bile creep up my throat.

I felt the familiar sway of that fir tree in Camarillo, but this time it didn't bring joy and a sense of belonging. My stomach churned, and I barely made it to the bushes in front of the apartment before I threw up. I gazed at the puddle of sick and wondered how I'd managed to convince myself this sort of behavior was right for me.

SURE ABOUT VIETNAM

A month after I puked in front of that man's apartment, I had something bigger to worry about. The Vietnam War was heating up, and like every other young man I knew, I had just received my draft number. It was low, and that meant after graduation in two years, I would be drafted into military service.

I figured God had given me that low number and wanted me to join the generation to which I was going to minister in the battle we'd been called to fight. Fatalities mounted by the day, and I figured I'd have a better chance of survival if I went to Vietnam as an officer instead of an enlisted man. To make that happen, I took the entrance exam for San Jose State's chapter of ROTC (Reserve Officer's Training Corps). Proud of myself for doing my duty (and in the safest way possible!), I shared my decision with my girlfriend, Jeanne, as we sat in my red Volkswagen Beetle outside my apartment.

We'd been a couple for two and a half years, and we planned to marry when I graduated. I told her I would sign the ROTC contract in the morning. I spoke in solemn tones about my responsibility to shoulder the burden of war.

She stayed silent for a long time. Then she pivoted in her seat, took my face in her hands, and said, "Are you sure you want to go kill people in a war you don't believe in?"

Her hands cradled my face, but it felt like I'd been slapped. I seized the gearshift knob and couldn't let go. I tried to look away but couldn't take my eyes off hers. I'd been so sure of my decision, and it had violated what I stood for.

SHOTS ACROSS THE BOW

I'm confused when my certainty about things turns out to be so wrong. What drives me in these situations? What contaminates the instincts I rely on to find my way forward? The spaciousness and generosity that emerged in me over years has been replaced with a deep suspicion of my own judgment and motives.

There's a crowd inside my head, pulling me this way and that. It's too confusing to sort out, too strange to trust. I can't admit how shaken I am, and an unnoticed insecurity drives me to even more misplaced certainty.

Chapter 3

THE COST OF DOUBLING DOWN

Age 20-22
I mistake belief for truth, behave badly
And take pride in doing so
Shame unfelt hardens into self-righteousness

RIGHT ABOUT THE CALL

It was a bright, cool, September morning. I'd started my second year at San Jose State, and as I waited for the stoplight at 4th and San Carlos streets, I experienced a "call." One moment, I wanted nothing more than to get to class on time, and the next, I wanted to be a priest. I didn't choose the vocation, thoughtfully selecting it over other options. I just awoke to the certainty that, somewhere inside me, the choice had already been made.

Furthermore, the choice was right: like swaying in that tree was right, like helping my little brother make a kite was right, like seeing the future before it happened in a Little League game was right: a rightness so compelling it never occurred to question the assumptions, convictions, and decisions that came with it.

In my imagination, the future rolled itself out, a red carpet of welcome. In three years, I would graduate from college, marry my high school sweetheart, spend another three years at an

Episcopal seminary, get ordained, serve for two years as an associate parish minister, and then have a congregation of my own to lead. I could relax and let it all play out.

That weekend, I told my parents about the call. Mom seemed pleased, Dad thoughtful, and when I walked into the kitchen for a glass of water, Dad followed. We stood at the far end of the green Formica table where, as a family, we'd shared so many meals. He spoke slowly, thoughtfully, and as usual, he led with something other than his main point.

"I was on jury duty last week."

"Yeah?"

"I couldn't take my eyes off the prosecutor. He was a young man, and he was so … good at what he did … so intelligent, so organized, so sure of himself."

He paused for a moment, and then he said it: "You'd have made a great lawyer."

My thoughts picked up speed. *He's disappointed I want to be a priest.*

Before I could react, he continued to muse. "You know, throughout our lives, we come to forks in the road; we make a choice, and that choice takes us one direction instead of another."

So ….

"When I finished high school in Charlottesville, I chose to go to college. There, I got interested in engineering. That led to work with Sperry Gyroscope in New York. Sperry sent me on a business trip to Bellingham, Washington, where I met and married your mother. Sperry moved us to Southern California, where I designed guidance systems for missiles. That work led to a job with Lockheed in San Jose, and along the way it led to having you three children."

"And your point is …"

"If I'd decided not to go to college, I'd have been a farmer in Virginia."

He paused, and I held my breath. This was way too arbitrary: the vast differences in futures because of one simple choice. My stomach flipped. *Am I deluding myself about being a priest, like I did about acting?*

"Dad," I said, "don't you think you were *meant* to be an engineer, meet Mom, live here ..."

I couldn't bring myself to add, "And have me?"

He put his hands on my shoulders, squeezed hard, and held my gaze. "No, I don't think that at all. You come to forks in the road, you make a choice, and that choice takes you here instead of there. And either way is fine."

I felt the sway again, but this time I froze. I looked past him at the refrigerator, the kitchen sink, the laminated cabinets. I couldn't make sense of what he had said. I didn't really think either way was fine. It was either one way or the other, and I had to be sure. I felt my jaw tighten. God had called me, and I was off to seminary.

Nothing was going to get in my way.

RIGHT ABOUT MY CHURCH

In 1957, when we moved from Camarillo to San Jose, we were one of the first families to join a new Episcopal congregation known as St. Andrew's. During the next ten years, I served as an acolyte, sang in several choirs, and joined the youth groups. I learned to play guitar and led the folk masses that were part of the church's liturgical reform.

St. Andrew's was the epitome of Episcopalian via media: a middle-of-the-road approach to Christianity that avoided the extremes of Roman Catholicism on the one hand and Evangelical

Protestantism on the other. The Episcopalians I knew believed in God but didn't go overboard. They maintained the Catholic liturgical tradition but had far less hierarchy and certainly no pope. The church honored the Bible but curated the Sunday Scripture readings to reflect the development of theological thought and the sweep of Christian history. They welcomed visitors but didn't knock on doors to find them. They rarely disclosed their personal beliefs, but they worked hard at building community and serving the less fortunate.

It was a progressive church, and it became well known in the San Francisco Bay Area. It hosted lectures from visiting scholars and media figures, ran a thrift store in a nearby village, and promoted Cursillo: an intensive weekend immersion into Christian life that originated in Spain and took hold in South America as part of the Christian Liberation movement.

In the years following my decision to be a priest, I got even more involved in St. Andrews. I led a Cursillo-type retreat for the youth. I attended a class on *The Phenomenon of Man*, the book by French theologian, Pierre Teilhard de Chardin, who integrated Christian Theology with the science of evolution. I joined local clergy for a spiritual development workshop with Henri Nouwen, whose passion and energy electrified me. I devoured books by our bishop, James Pike. I especially remember, *A Time for Christian Candor*.

The Eucharist moved me. When I received the bread and wine, the moment expanded, and I sensed a connection with something larger than myself. That connection, and my sense of being part of a long history of theological thought, was enough to get me to seminary.

I had found my place, far from the competitive and confusing world of business, politics, and other professions where you had to make your own way. Church was my home away from home. As one of its priests, I would be set for life.

RIGHT ABOUT LYING

In late May 1969, I stood in the bedroom of my college apartment and packed a final box of books. The previous six years had been tumultuous and frightening. The normal teenage struggles had been amplified by the Vietnam War and the assassinations of John F. Kennedy, Malcolm X, Martin Luther King, Jr., and Robert Kennedy.

In a few weeks, I would leave the chaos and pain behind: graduate, get married, and head for Virginia. Two days earlier, I attended my last class: a course in philosophical logic which I didn't understand, judged irrelevant to daily existence, and had barely shown up for.

The phone on my desk rang, and it was the professor of that class.

"I'm reading everyone's final paper, but I don't see yours."

Shit! I'd never written it and thought him so dull he wouldn't notice.

"Well, I turned it in." The lie slithered out. My body tingled. I felt tall.

"When?"

"Tuesday morning." The second lie was easy.

"What time."

I held my breath and took a chance. "About 8:30."

The long pause was torturous.

"I'd stepped out for a quick meeting."

"Well, I slid it under your door." The story expanded. I was on a roll.

"I can't give you a passing grade unless I have a paper from you."

I went on the offensive. "That's not fair. I'm packing up my apartment, I graduate in two weeks, I get married, and I'm off to seminary." That last word was the closer. After all, I was going to be a priest.

"I've got to have a paper."

"Well, how about I whip something up now. It won't be much. My books are all packed …"

"I can't give you any more than a "C" for that."

"Fine. I'll get it to you this afternoon."

An hour later, I walked the paper to his office, put it in his hands, and said, "It's all I can do at the last moment."

I had successfully bluffed my way around this speed bump that stood between me and my God-given destiny. I had stood up for my call to be a priest against a nitpicking bureaucrat whose class, to begin with, was such a drag.

I had lied to his face, and it didn't bother me at all.

RIGHT ABOUT LEAVING

Jeanne and I were married in the early afternoon of June 28, 1969. We'd been together five years and were more than ready to start our new life with my entrance into Virginia Theological Seminary. Our honeymoon would be our trip across country, and we decided to take in as many sights as possible. We gave our destinations to AAA, and they provided eleven guidebooks that highlighted our route in green: a zigzag from San Jose to Alexandria. We packed our belongings—clothes, a small bookcase, and wedding gifts—and arranged storage with Mayflower Van Lines. We outfitted our new VW camper with a small Weber barbecue and the staples required to cook our own meals. Ten days ahead of schedule, we were ready to go.

The next morning was a Thursday, and courtesy of too much drink the night before, I lay on the living room couch, willing myself to do something productive. The phone rang. On the other end of the line, my brother was weeping. "Dad's dead," he choked. He stumbled through the story. John, Dad, Mom, and my sister, Sally, were playing golf. Dad collapsed on the seventh tee. John drove the car onto the golf course. They raced to the hospital: Sally in the front seat, Mom in the back with Dad's head on her lap. Dad was breathing when they arrived, but he died a few minutes later. The three of them were still at the hospital.

I said we'd leave right away. We got there fifteen minutes later and caught them just as they were leaving.

"We waited as long as we could," Mom said. "We just didn't know when the two of you would make it."

"I told John fifteen minutes." I raised my watch to prove the point, and Jeanne tightened her grip on my arm.

"Well, we're leaving," Mom said. "This is no place to talk about … what just happened. You can join us at home, unless you have something more important to do."

I bit back what I wanted to say. My parents and I had a difficult few months leading up to the wedding. I spent my weekends with Jeanne instead of them, and we had numerous fights about it. I'd even made it okay with myself to leave right after the generous rehearsal dinner they'd hosted in our family home. Instead of helping with the cleanup, I took Jeanne out for drinks with our friends. At our wedding the next day, we all put on a brave face, but we were tense around each other.

And now, Dad was gone.

Soon after we got to the house, our parish priest, Roy Strasburger, arrived. He and his assistant, West Davis, were my role models for the priesthood, and Strasburger had taken me under his wing. He was tall, Texan, and loved nicknames. Years earlier, he'd crowned us Big Roy and Little Roy. Now, he sat in our living room, at ease in Dad's favorite chair. My brother and sister perched on the brick hearth, Jeanne and I huddled on the couch, and Mom drifted in and out of the kitchen, bearing cookies and coffee.

Cookies and coffee?

Big Roy kept up a constant patter.

"Mary, this coffee is wonderful."

"Oh, Roy, it's just instant."

"Just instant? But it has so much flavor."

"Yes, it's wonderful what they can do these days."

A moment of panic tightened my gut. *Is this what I'll be doing the rest of my life?*

To Roy's credit, he eventually directed the conversation to things that mattered: which mortuary to use, who needed to be contacted, and he scheduled Dad's service for the following week. He kept the conversation light and steady, and Mom hung on his every word.

I sat frozen with disgust while Jeanne ferried plates to and from the kitchen. She didn't seem affected by the weirdness. I wondered if scenes like this were familiar to her. Her folks were farmer stock from Missouri, and whenever anyone died, the clan gathered around casseroles and talked about how the loved one was now "in a better place."

I finally used Big Roy's presence as an excuse to leave. Mom's twin sister, Sarah, would arrive tomorrow. Thankfully, Dad's service wouldn't delay our trip to Virginia. There was nothing for me to do, and the entire scene made my skin crawl. Mom's goodbye was frosty. Brother John looked lost, and sister Sally couldn't lift her eyes from the floor. I promised to return the next day, took Jeanne by the hand, and left as quickly as I could.

The next morning, I invented things to do and delayed our return until one o'clock. When we arrived, the front door was unlocked, but I rang the bell and waited. John quietly opened the door and whispered, "God, I'm glad you're here. Watch out.

Aunt Sarah's on the warpath."

We all knew Aunt Sarah's ability to stir the pot. She was a critical, judgmental, and demanding presence, and when she eventually died from cancer of the tongue, I uncharitably thought it poetic justice.

I thanked John for the warning and exchanged a glance with Jeanne. I braced myself, and we walked into the kitchen. Mom and Sarah were at the sink, scrubbing dishes as if typhoid was on the loose. They saw us come into the room but didn't say hello.

"Can I help?" Jeanne offered.

Mom stayed silent. Sarah glanced left and right, as if it were obvious there was no room for Jeanne. "No," she snapped. "If you'd been here earlier, you could have pitched in, but now you're too late."

Jeanne looked at the stack of dried dishes on the kitchen table and said, "Perhaps if I put these away."

"You don't know where they go," said Sarah, head down, scrubbing away.

Jeanne was diplomatic and didn't mention the many times over the years she had helped clean up after a meal. Instead, she addressed Mom directly.

"Mary, is there anything I can do?"

Sarah whipped her head in our direction, face aflame and lips drawn. "No! You two don't have to do anything. You just go on your merry way, off to seminary." The word was an accusation.

My stomach cramped. We were on a tight timeline. Our journey was carefully planned to the day. We'd visit places we'd never been and arrive in Alexandria just in time to find an apartment, secure a job for Jeanne, and prepare for school. Yes, we could delay our departure, abandon our sightseeing, and make a beeline for Virginia, but this was our honeymoon, *our* time. And, after all, we'd make it to Dad's service before we left.

"Aunt Sarah," I said, "we have ten days before we go."

"You think this'll blow over in ten days? You two live in your own little world, don't you? You don't care about anyone but yourselves. If you were my son ..."

"Well, I'm not your son." *Thank God.*

She turned to Jeanne, quiet, polite Jeanne, who never said anything to ruffle feathers.

"You just go ahead and be selfish. Take him away from his family who needs him; just run off to Virginia and leave the rest of us to pick up the pieces."

Jeanne's jaw dropped, and her eyes filled with tears.

"Goddammit, Sarah," I growled. "Back off."

Mom finally spoke. "Wesley Roy Whitten, show some respect for your aunt. She's my sister, and ..." She broke into tears. "She's all I have now."

Mom sobbed, and Sarah took her in her arms. I grabbed Jeanne and stormed out of the kitchen. Behind me, I heard Mom cry harder. Sarah said something to her I couldn't hear and didn't want to. I felt my hand on Jeanne's arm and worried I was squeezing too hard.

John stopped us in the living room. "What the hell was that?"

"Look, this place is fucking crazy. I'm getting as far away from here as possible, and you should too, just as soon as you can."

On the way out, I slammed the door.

Dad's funeral was eight days later, and I insisted on reading the New Testament lesson from 1 Corinthians 13. When I climbed into the lectern, I looked down at my mother. Her face was a mask of pain. I looked out at the congregation and was surprised at the number of people. The church held 450, and nearly every seat was taken. I had no idea Dad was so popular.

As I read the words, "When I became a man, I gave up childish ways," I felt confirmed in my decision to leave home and start my own family: one without all the drama and pressure to conform. I didn't feel shock or grief, just a burning desire to get the hell away.

THE LURE OF CERTAINTY

I'm reminded of Eric Hoffer's 1951 book in which he defines a "true believer" as someone who seeks certainty and simplicity to escape the burdens of freedom and individuality. Grief, anger, and defensiveness contaminate what otherwise are genuine impulses toward something transcendent and life-giving.

Much later in life, on January 6th, I would see the destructive power of "true believerism" in others. At this moment, I'm the one caught in the dynamic. In the face of things I can't control, I take comfort in being right.

But there's such a thing as being "dead right," and a reckoning is on the way.

Chapter 4

CORRECTION TIME

Age 23-24
My sell-out to certainty is confronted by events
I'm not wise enough to want
It requires a lot to break through the lies
That prop me up in the dark

A DEATH APPLAUDED

At 7:30 in the morning on September 3, 1969, I sat in the third row of the chapel at Virginia Theological Seminary. It was the first week of graduate school, and we started each day with Morning Prayer. I needed the service that morning, because the man who had confirmed me into the Episcopal Church had just died, alone, in the Judean Desert.

James Albert Pike, the Bishop of California, came to the priesthood later in life, after working as a lawyer and intelligence officer for the Navy. He was my bishop, and not just in name only. He actively supported Martin Luther King Jr. and the civil rights movement, advocated for women's rights, endorsed gender equality for what was then known as the gay and lesbian community, and championed people from all walks of life to become priests in his diocese.

He wrote many books, two of which were bestsellers. He

brooked no bullshit, and he continually challenged orthodox beliefs not based on data and experience: the Trinity, the Virgin Birth, the Incarnation, Dogmatic Authority, and the physical resurrection of Jesus. He focused on the importance of not just telling the truth but doing the truth. I once heard him say, "The problem with church is that people can receive a dose of Christianity which inoculates them against the real thing."

In 1966, when I completed my first year in college and began my second, Pike's life was upended. In February, his son committed suicide. In May, he submitted his resignation as Bishop of California to the Episcopal House of Bishops who ratified it in September. Pike became a theologian-in-residence at the Center for the Study of Democratic Institutions in Santa Barbara. Two weeks later, a group of conservative bishops circulated a petition accusing him of heresy. Pike demanded an ecclesiastical trial to clear his name, but the House of Bishops, fearing negative publicity, chose to censure him instead. In November, eight years after he welcomed me into the Episcopal Church, Time magazine featured him in its cover story, titled, "Religion: Heretic or Prophet?"

Three years later, during the weeks Jeanne and I drove across country to Virginia, Pike and his third wife, Diane, traveled to the Holy Land. They decided to follow Jesus' example and "enter the wilderness." Their car got stuck in a ditch and stranded them deep in the desert. They set out on foot for Qumran, the home of the Dead Sea Scrolls. They walked in the wrong direction, and, after long hours in the brutal heat, Jim Pike collapsed. Diane set out alone, looking for help, and stumbled across a camp of Arab laborers who organized a search party. They found Pike's body at the base of a cliff in the Wadi Masash.

At the start of Morning Prayer, newly installed dean, Cecil Woods stood at the top of the steps leading to the choir stalls and announced the death of "the disgraced bishop." Many of my classmates applauded, and a few even cheered. The "heretic" had died, and I was sure they saw it as a demonstration of God's justice, a vindication of the status quo. Dad's death, just two months earlier, roared back to life, and my heart ached in protest. I kept quiet, but I felt a tear run down my cheek as I tried to take a breath.

What the hell had happened to the Episcopal Church I knew and loved? I was 3,000 miles from home, committed to a future that included people who openly celebrated the death of a man whose life had fueled my desire to become a priest. Yes, Pike had been abrasive, argumentative, and dismissive of orthodoxy, but he advocated for the rights of others, and he stood for telling the truth and being inclusive. And these people with whom I was in seminary were celebrating his demise.

How would I study with them, be ordained with them, and serve alongside them in the church? How great was their number, and did I really want to spend my life fighting them? I wanted to walk out of the chapel, get in my car, and drive back to California.

The dean said nothing about the outburst, and he continued with the service as if nothing unusual had taken place. I looked at the open Book of Common Prayer in my hands, and the words swam on the page. I took a deep breath, my thoughts came to a standstill, and I made a decision.

I would excel at my studies. I knew how to do that, and I'd use what I learned to rescue my religion from the grasp of people who would cheer the passing of someone who dared to be different. Challenging the status quo was a key element of Jesus' life, and I would follow his example.

I belonged here. I was going to stay, I was going to learn, and I was going to beat them at their own game.

AN ASS-KICKING

The following Monday morning, I was back in the chapel for week two of my seminary career. By now, I knew my way around. The chapel sat at the eastern end of the seminary's 80-acre campus. It stood adjacent to Aspinwall Hall, the red brick, Colonial structure that anchored one end of a long, oval drive that encircled a lush lawn studded with oak trees.

At the end of this morning's service, Dean Woods made another announcement.

"Two weeks ago, before he resigned, a matter about which we will not speak at present, Dr. Trotter, our former dean, put into place an educational experiment that I didn't have time to cancel. It is referred to as 'sensitivity training,' whatever that may be, and you will spend the next two weekends participating in 'T-groups,' whatever they are. At the close of service, you are to proceed across the oval to the refectory, where you will be given an orientation. It won't last long. The faculty has made it clear we don't want your first period New Testament class to be compromised any more than absolutely necessary."

At the orientation we were sorted into groups of eight and introduced to our T-group "facilitators." We were told to attend class as usual for the next four days. On Friday after chapel, we were to report to our T-group locations, where we would spend three days, 15 hours a day, "in training." Friday morning arrived, and, after chapel, my eight-person group walked to our assigned meeting room: the lounge, just outside the refectory doors. The facilitators asked us to move the overstuffed chairs, long sofas, and end tables away from the center of the room. This exposed a large area over which sat a Persian rug.

"Have a seat," said Jim Fenhagen, the rector of St. John's, Georgetown, and the male half of the facilitation team. He indicated with a sweep of his hand that we were to sit on the rug, in a circle. He and his co-facilitator, a woman named Liz, sat at either end of the circle, while the eight of us students chatted about the first week of classes. Eventually, we noticed Jim and Liz weren't speaking. They sat there and watched us. We quieted down, and they stayed silent, for a long time.

Finally, Liz asked, "Who'd like to share?"

As the hours passed, it became clear there was no formal agenda: no lectures, notes, papers, or tests. You were free to feel what you felt, say what you thought, and use any language you wished. You couldn't be violent, but you could get angry, even insult other members of the group, but whatever you said was open to challenge. You had to explain what you meant, identify your assumptions, express yourself clearly, and listen to how what you said affected others.

The operating imperative was to be authentic instead of false, to connect with each other instead of pushing others away— and this required self-awareness. Soon, it became clear why this experience was called "sensitivity" or "encounter" training: you increased your sensitivity to others by encountering your own prejudices, assumptions, and pretense.

I was wary but confident I'd stand out in this setting. After all, I was from California and used to small group work.

Five hours into our first day, I felt enraged with one of my classmates. "Al" was everything I never wanted to be. Whenever he spoke, he tilted his head back, cleared his throat several times, and made small circles with his right hand, as if winding himself up. When he finally opened his mouth, he sounded like a character out of Dickens. What was the matter with this guy? He just didn't fit in. He wasn't … normal.

The next morning, Jim asked Al a question, and once again Al hemmed and hawed and twirled his hand.

I exploded. "Goddammit, Al, just spit it out!" I laughed and looked at the group. I expected them to laugh along with me. I'd timed the comment perfectly, and surely everyone was as exasperated with this guy as I was. But nobody chuckled, nobody smiled. Everyone just stared … at me.

After a long, awkward moment, Liz spoke in a calm voice. "Roy, it sounds like you have something you want to say to Al. Why don't you say it straight instead of hiding it with sarcasm and humor?"

My face was on fire. As I gazed at the rug in front of me, I heard someone whisper, "Oh, my God." The silence lingered.

I reached for something truthful to say. "Al, everything about you just drives me crazy."

I expected the roof to fall in, but Liz simply said, "Thank you for sharing."

She turned to Al, "And what do you want to say to Roy?"

"Well," Al paused: more throat-clearing, twirling, waiting for words. "I don't think it's my fault you feel that way."

"Sure, pin it on me, you bastard." The words flew out before I could stop them.

"You sound like you're gearing up for a fight," said Liz.

I couldn't think of anything to say back.

"So," she persisted, "*Do* you feel like fighting?"

No one had ever asked me that before, and strangely, it settled me down.

"Well, I guess I do."

"Fine. How do you want to fight?"

I had an idea. I'd wrestled one semester in high school physical education, and for a year in college, I'd studied competitive judo with the Olympic gold medal team at San Jose State.

"How about we wrestle?" I didn't think Al would go for it, I'd win by default, and the focus of discussion would pass to someone else.

"Well," Al said slowly, "If Roy wants to wrestle, I guess we could do that."

I quickly sized him up. He was two inches taller, and his shoulders were broad, but he was a bookworm and a social misfit. I could take him.

"All right," said Jim. "Let's make some room."

The group spread out and created a large space in the middle of the carpet.

Jesus. We're going to do this, I thought.

"Let's warm up a moment," said Al.

Warm up? I was right about this guy. What a wuss.

I got to my feet and stretched a little, but Al had a routine: neck rolls, shoulder stretches, twists for his back and legs, and finally a full neck bridge. When he arched his back, balancing on his feet and neck, the group applauded, and several people laughed out loud.

Hmm.

Al dropped out of his bridge, shook his body a final time, and said, "I'll start on top."

I knew what "top" and "bottom" meant in competitive wrestling, but I had a plan: I'd reverse him, and this would be over in a minute.

"Sounds like you know what you're doing," Liz said to Al. "Have you wrestled before?"

"Four years, in college." Al replied.

Oh, crap.

I knelt on all fours, Al grabbed my right bicep, hard, and wrapped his other hand firmly around my stomach. I heard Jim count down from three, and suddenly I was face-down on the mat feeling Al's full weight on my back. I twisted, turned, hooked one of his legs, then the other, pulled his right arm under and tried to roll. He countered everything.

I got angry, and then, I panicked. I kicked, twisted, and bucked with everything I had. I threw him off and got to my feet. Now, we were face-to-face, and I was ready to throw him. But before I could make a move, Al leapt. He put me on my back, pinned my shoulders to the carpet, and the group counted me out. He let me go, and I crawled to my feet. I grumbled that the count was unfair: my shoulders hadn't really been down, and I'd been about to break free. Liz let my comments pass unremarked and suggested we "close up the circle and reflect on what happened."

Before calling on Al and me, she asked everyone else to speak. My face burned even hotter, and I listened with my head down, staring at the blue and gold threads that wove their way through the carpet. The students shared how surprised they'd been at Al's skill. Clearly, he'd gone up a notch in their estimation. I longed for a good word or two about myself, but I really didn't expect it. I'd been a jerk, gotten my ass kicked, and didn't deserve any praise.

When it was Al's turn to speak, he let us know his college wrestling team had won the state finals the spring before he entered seminary. *What an idiot I'd been!* Then, he turned to me and said, "And you were a tough opponent."

I thought for a moment he was mocking me, but he added, "I mean it. Not a lot of people escape from that first hold I had on you."

My eyes filled, and something gave way in my chest. I looked at Al and saw a strength and a gentleness I hadn't seen before. I felt the sway of the fir tree, and, after an hour or two, humiliation gave way to a sense of belonging.

A LESSON IN CRAZY

As we neared the end of our first year at seminary, each

student was summoned to an interview for CPE: Clinical Pastoral Education. We were to spend the entire summer in a full-time program that combined pastoral work with self-development.

CPE had recently been added to the curriculum, an educational reform instituted years earlier by the former dean, Jess Trotter. It was practice, not theory, and there was a narrow range of available postings. The most desirable jobs were as aides to senators and congressional representatives: not much pastoral work, but a lot of self-development. There were a few slots at schools or hospitals. I was assigned to what the student rumor mill deemed the bottom of the barrel: a chaplaincy at Spring Grove Mental Hospital in Catonsville, Maryland.

When I arrived at the hospital that first morning, I was placed in a cohort with three students from other seminaries and a clinical supervisor named Bob Olson. We spent the morning introducing ourselves and sharing our reservations about working with what we called, "crazy people." The four of us had lunch together in the hospital cafeteria, and instead of returning to our meeting room, Bob told us to put on our clerical collars and head for the locked wards.

I stood outside the door of the men's ward to which I'd been assigned. I heard the door buzz, I felt my collar scraping my neck, and I noticed my hand shook as I opened the door and walked into the room. The door slammed shut behind me, and I heard screaming. I turned, and a young man with bulging eyes and flying hair stumbled toward me: "You, you're the one who stole my fifty-thousand dollars!"

A huge attendant, dressed in white, charged out of the nurse's station and wrapped his arms around the man, bringing him to a halt just three feet from where I stood.

"Now, Billy," the attendant crooned, "I want to introduce you to someone special. This is Chaplain Roy. You'd like to say hello to Chaplain Roy, wouldn't you, Billy?"

Billy smiled broadly. Several teeth were missing. He pointed at my collar and put his hands together as if he were praying. He bowed, and in a singsong voice, said, "Oh yes, Chaplain Roy, how very nice to meet you."

The attendant walked Billy back to the nurses' station, where another man in a white coat held a needle. He gave Billy a shot and took him to the rear of the room, laid him on a bed, and left him alone to sleep off the drug. I guessed they'd been through this before with Billy.

I hovered near the door and arranged my face to look calm and unbothered. I'd been in the ward for just a couple of minutes, but I was sure of one thing: itchy neck or not, I would wear this damn collar every day for the rest of the summer. Eventually, I moved into the ward and tried to talk to people who weren't spinning in circles or staring catatonically into space. Several of them couldn't or didn't want to speak, but I did find a couple of men who filled the time telling me how they'd landed in Spring Grove. Their stories were disturbingly "normal": no dramatic episodes of abuse or violence, just an accumulation of experiences they couldn't handle.

Five days a week, for all thirteen weeks of summer "vacation," that was my routine. In the afternoons, I worked with patients, and in the mornings, I worked on myself. I read books like *Portnoy's Complaint, One Flew Over the Cuckoo's Nest,* and *The Fifty-Minute Hour.* I saw training films like *Three Approaches to Psychotherapy,* in which the same mental patient, Gloria Szymanski, underwent three therapy sessions: with Albert Ellis, Fritz Perls, and Carl Rogers. Each therapist demonstrated his approach to healing mental trauma.

In college, I'd been bored by the psychology I studied, but this stuff fascinated me. I spent my afternoons practicing one therapeutic methodology after another. I learned to sit in silence with patients who were quiet and to follow with curiosity the long and winding stories of those who longed to be heard. I had moments of chickening out, like with Emily on the women's ward who spent hours spinning in circles. I thought to mimic her, spin with her, and see where it would lead, but I couldn't risk appearing odd. I sat in a chair, watched her spin, and hated myself for looking good instead of following my instincts.

All of us student chaplains made mistakes. We listened too long or said too much, we avoided people we feared and clung to those with whom we felt comfortable. But no matter how often we goofed, these patients, who had already suffered so much, would give us another chance. Some of them were so far gone they would likely spend the rest of their days in a place like this. Some were con artists, especially those who'd been institutionalized instead of sent to prison, and they repeatedly asked for favors, for cash, for anything they could get.

But the majority were just ordinary human beings who'd been through trauma that had brought them to their knees. Often, they were far more honest and authentic than any of us who were doing our best to stand alongside them. They'd been through hell, and they were doing the best they could with what they had.

Those were the people who got through to me. All I could do for them was listen and learn what life had been like for them. I spent the next-to-last day of my CPE experience back in the men's ward where I'd started. I noticed how calm I felt as I talked to the patients, even with Billy who patted my chest as he said hello. I listened more than I talked.

I was no longer afraid, and I learned something that changed my life. All these people were troubled, but they weren't the only crazy ones in the room. I had problems too. On the last day of my CPE experience, I asked Bob Olson if I could see him professionally. He agreed to take me into counseling.

On the long drive home from Baltimore, my friends had much to say about their summer experience. I shared little. Mostly, I just felt myself rock back and forth in the car seat. It had been quite a summer.

A NARROW ESCAPE

In September 1970, I started my second year of seminary. By October, the counseling I received from Bob Olson revealed how competitive I'd been with my classmates. I'd spent the previous year securing top grades and faculty attention. When some of the professors remarked on my potential as a scholar, I was confident the year had been a success.

CPE and my therapy, however, opened my eyes to how I'd contributed to my family's dysfunction and revealed the lies I told myself to make tolerable the loneliness I'd felt for years. Now, I hungered for two things: I wanted to be honest, and I wanted deeper relationships with my peers.

For the first time, I noticed the words carved into the stone arch over the door to the seminary library: "Seek the truth, come whence it may, cost what it will." Soon thereafter, I read a diocesan newsletter about the latest convention of our church. When the author of the article listened to one of the bishops speak, he wrote three words in his notebook: "Straight, straight, straight!" I wanted somebody, someday to write those words about me.

Over the next several months, I worked hard to make new friends and express the truth of what I felt and thought. When I didn't see the relevance to modern ministry of what we were being taught, I spoke up rather than wait and see if there was something I didn't yet understand. This increased my popularity among my peers, but it alienated several teachers.

At a counseling session in March, when I reported all this to Bob Olson, along with my doubts about whether I was cut out for the parish ministry, he floated the idea of an intern year to "test my vocation." My chest relaxed, and I decided an intern year was exactly what I needed.

I interviewed at nearly every Episcopal church in the greater Washington, D.C. area to see if I could secure a position, at minimum salary, for the following year. I had 22 interviews in three weeks.

The day after I returned to school, Sid Sanders, the seminary chaplain, in whom I'd confided my doubts, pulled me aside after lunch.

"I probably shouldn't be telling you this, but I want to give you a heads-up. Your mid-seminary review is on Monday, and the faculty is going to ask you to leave."

"They're kicking me out?"

Sid placed a hand on my shoulder.

"I know this is difficult for you, but you've got to admit you've been hard to live with this year."

He paused, and I pounced.

"What? They can't take a little disagreement. This is just revenge for my speaking up in class."

Sid raised his voice. "Look, you haven't been in class for three weeks now. What the hell were you thinking?"

The irony was overwhelming. I told Sid I'd decided to take an intern year, and I'd been interviewing for a position.

"Why didn't you tell us that's what you were doing?"

"I thought I had to handle it on my own."

"It would have helped to know that when we discussed you last week. Several of us spoke on your behalf, but you were nowhere to be found. The dean said you're too immature for the ministry, and his opinion carried the day."

My face went numb. Deciding to take a year out and working to find a job was one of the most mature things I'd ever done. I couldn't win.

"Listen," Sid said, "I'll take your side on Monday, but you'd better be prepared for the worst."

The weekend brought little relief. I heard from a dozen of the priests I'd interviewed, all of whom informed me they weren't interested. Jeanne knew about the intern year, but not that the faculty wanted to kick me out of school. I was too embarrassed to tell her the truth. I avoided any discussion about seminary and hoped against hope that things would work out.

On Monday morning, I stood in the vestibule outside the large conference room where the faculty had gathered for the day's Middler Reviews. Sid came out of the room and told me they would be ready for me in 15 minutes. He looked sad.

Just then, a secretary came through the door and said Roland Jones at Church of the Ascension in Silver Spring had called and asked me to phone as soon as possible. There was a pay phone in the vestibule. I called, and Roland offered me a job. I hung up the phone and bent over, hands on my knees. Tears puddled on the floor. Five minutes later, Sid escorted me into the meeting.

Dean Woods greeted me coolly and asked me to stand at the lectern in front of the assembled professors. Some of the faculty looked sorrowful. A few of them glared at me, and the rest of them found something fascinating in their laps. In a sonorous voice, rich with a soft Virginia drawl, Dean Woods informed me they were terribly sorry, it had been a difficult decision, but they thought it best if I would consider not returning in the fall.

That was Virginia-speak for "Don't let the door smack you in the ass on the way out." I went on offense. "Actually, I agree with you."

The Dean rocked back on his heels, the professors perked up, and with all the smoothness I could muster, I kept talking.

"As a couple of you know"—I nodded at Sid and John Woolverton, professor of church history, who had taken an interest in my welfare—"I've been in therapy since the start of the year. A month ago, I came to the same conclusion you did: that I lacked experience. And that's why you haven't seen me in class during the past three weeks. I've been setting up an intern year."

I paused for dramatic effect.

"I interviewed with 22 rectors in the Washington, D.C. area, and I've been hired by Roland Jones in Silver Spring."

I didn't look at Dean Woods. The faculty were my audience now, and most of them were smiling. I heard the dean clear his throat, and I kept talking before he could intervene.

"So, in September, I'll begin my intern year as a non-ordained associate at Church of the Ascension. I'll stay in touch with Sid, if that's all right with you, and make sure he receives regular reports from Roland on my progress. And, pending a successful completion of the year, I'll return next fall and complete my degree. How's that sound?"

They applauded, and I snuck a glance at the dean who not only had his hands at his side but looked as if he'd been slapped in the face. I waited for the applause to die down. Cecil Woods accepted the verdict of the assembled group and said he would look forward to receiving Sid's reports. I walked out before anyone could change their mind.

The next day, John Woolverton pulled me aside. We had history. He was one of the professors whose field of study I had questioned. I had confronted him in class about the value of learning church history. His answer was succinct: "You learn history to avoid the mistakes of previous generations." I stopped complaining. He'd been right, and he was about to be right again.

"You thought you got away with something in there, didn't you?"

"It was a test, and I passed."

"No, it was a narrow escape."

He looked me in the eyes, and the penny dropped. It was what Sid had been trying to tell me, what I was too blind to see. I'd behaved like nobody cared about me, like I was on my own, like the faculty wasn't for me, but against me. That defensive posture had been a way of life since junior high school.

"I didn't realize that, John."

He smiled. "I know." Then he offered Jeanne and me their home for the summer while he and his wife, Maggie, vacationed in Martha's Vineyard.

"This will save you some money." He patted me on the shoulder.

And two months later, when he handed me his house keys, he said, "Have a good year, and learn to soft pedal things a bit."

SHOCKS TO THE SYSTEM

These two years present significant blows to my ego. I've plenty of hubris left, but I no longer trust my certainty about things. I lie to myself, a lot, and I don't even know I'm doing it. And those lies compromise how I see myself, and how I regard others.

I want something more for myself: to spend less time currying favor and competing and more time learning what I and others are really like. I'm surprised how few people are out to get me. There are some who'd like me to disappear—the dean is one of them—but there are so many who are kind, generous, and supportive.

Lies form a cage. It takes a lot of rattling to loosen the bars.

PASSAGE II

GRACE, RISK, AND RETREAT

1972-1981 — AGE 25-34

The unexpected and the uncanny
Evoke the courage to explore and take a stand

There's a relationship between what happens to me and what I need to learn. I begin to trust the former and assume my responsibility for the latter. It takes me to unknown places and delivers unexpected gifts.

Chapter 5

NECESSARY GIFTS

Age 25
The right gift at the right moment
Unearned and required

GIVEN A CHANCE

In late August 1971, Jeanne and I moved to Maryland and rented an apartment across the street from Church of the Ascension in Silver Spring. A week later, I stuck a thin sliver of black electrical tape on my clerical collar, indicating I wasn't yet ordained, and went to work as almost-an-associate priest.

Roland Jones assigned me to preach on my first Sunday at the church. He gave me three weeks' notice, and I started to prepare. I found a book of Peter Marshall's sermons from his tenure as chaplain to the U.S. Senate. Marshall arranged his text in uneven lines, like poetry. From my first glance at the page, I felt the flow and cadence of his words. This layout of phrases and rhythm: this was how I thought, how I spoke, and how I could write to express not only my thoughts, but my feelings.

The congregation warmly welcomed us. They were a wonderful group of people, and the sermon went over well. Roland asked me to preach every other week for the rest of the year. He set me up in a makeshift office in the prop room behind the stage in the parish hall. The room was long and narrow. The half nearest the door had two chairs, a sofa, and a coffee table. Beyond them was a small desk. He apologized for the surroundings, but I was over the moon. My own office!

During the year, Roland made sure I had exposure to the full range of a parish minister's life. I called on newcomers, led the youth group, visited the sick, and provided pastoral counseling, mainly for the youth. I led the church's first folk mass, took a youth choir to perform at the National Cathedral, and even watched over the church eleven months later when Roland took vacation.

His generosity extended to a warm review of my work, even though after one sermon, he made a wry comment about my preaching the Gospel of Sigmund Freud instead of the Gospel of Jesus Christ. His report paved the way for a return to seminary for my final year.

I'd succeeded in my role at Ascension, and I was confident I could succeed as a parish minister in the Episcopal Church. I had nine months to learn the rest of what I needed for my future career, and I was about to find, perhaps to be found by, the finest teacher I ever encountered.

GIVEN AN UNDERSTANDING

In early September 1972, I returned to the seminary chapel and sat once again in my favorite pew: third row, on the Epistle side of the middle aisle. I waited for Morning Prayer to kick off my senior year. This was no ordinary day. The scheduled preacher was Dr. Jess Trotter, the former dean who had disappeared for three years following the suicide of his son.

Trotter was Dean of VTS from 1957 to his disappearance in 1969, just weeks before I entered seminary. He successfully led the school through the turbulence of the sixties. He helped the seminary wake up to its racism, its patriarchy, and its conventional approach to training people for ministry. He instituted Clinical Pastoral Education as a curriculum requirement, and, in one of his last acts as dean, he launched the T-group training experiment that had been so influential in my development.

The word had spread; by his own choice, Jess wouldn't return as dean, but as a professor of Systematic Theology, the focus of my last year of study. I was eager to hear from this man, whose educational leadership had made a significant difference in my life. I wondered if he would talk about the death of his son and how he had dealt with such a blow.

The organist launched into the opening hymn, we rose to our feet, and the clergy processed from the sacristy into the choir pews. Dr. Trotter was easy to spot; he was the only faculty person I didn't know. He wore the black cassock and white surplice favored by this "low church" seminary, and I was shocked to see how much he resembled my father: average height, glasses, thinning hair, somewhat overweight, and emanating a quiet vitality. Until that moment, I hadn't noticed that he too was named, "Jess."

After the sermon hymn, Dr. Trotter climbed into the pulpit, and he did indeed talk about his son. "My relationship with John had been very difficult for some time. He started using drugs, and I didn't know what to do. Whatever I tried just made things worse. We fought a lot, and I said and did things I deeply regret."

He choked up and paused a moment.

"One day, I came home for lunch, and John and I had yet another argument. We yelled, we covered familiar ground, and we resolved nothing. He stormed off to his room. Marnie and I heard a shot. We ran upstairs, and John died in our arms."

The silence in the chapel was total and terrible. I couldn't take my eyes off Dr. Trotter, and I couldn't stop thinking about Dad. My heart ached for this man who'd lost his son, and I hoped Dad's final thoughts included how much I loved him.

"In that moment," Dr. Trotter continued, "and in the days that followed, I thought about everything I'd accomplished, believed, and taught. None of it really helped. All of it was right, but it wasn't right enough to help me lose my son and carry on. What I believed, how I prayed, the way I lived—none of it enabled me to put my arms around what had happened."

I stared at the faculty. Some of them were rapt with attention, others looked like they'd rather be somewhere, anywhere else.

"That's why I left," Trotter continued. "And that was the beginning of finding my way back to a relationship with God that was truthful enough, real enough, and tough enough to call me into a future that no longer included my son alive and well. And that's why I'm returning to teaching this morning. I want to help you learn how, in your moments of tragedy and fear and doubt, to go into and through the pain you feel."

Tears ran down my face. I was glued to the pew.

Dr. Trotter looked up from his notes, gazed directly at us, and said, "Gentlemen, I have been to the bottom ... and the bottom is firm."

GIVEN AN EDUCATION

The next day, I met one-on-one with Dr. Trotter, who insisted we call each other by our first names. He asked a lot of questions about what I had found valuable in my first two years of study and what application it had to real ministry during my intern year.

At the end of our conversation, he recommended I spend the year studying Paul Tillich. "He's the last of the great philosophical theologians," he said, "and I think you'll find him a kindred soul."

I left Jess' office, walked to the library, checked out several books by and about Tillich, and claimed a carrel on the second floor as my study spot for the year. An hour later, librarian Jack Goodwin came by to say hello, inquire about my intern year, and wish me well. He suggested I keep a "daybook" to record what I read and what it inspired in my thinking. This was the start of a journal I've kept ever since.

Later that month, Professor John Rodgers introduced our class to a theological concept adorned with a weighty name: "theo-thanatology." In the 1950s and '60s, professional theologians coined the term to account for the rise of secularity in the West and the abandonment of traditional beliefs in God.

Time magazine covered its emergence in April 1966 and placed three words on its cover: Is God Dead? Theothanatology became known as The Death of God, a term borrowed from Nietzsche. Predictably, *Time's* coverage popularized this theological concept and diluted its impact. Rogers introduced it as a footnote, not a major development, in theological thought.

For me, however, it was a revelation. These theologians made a critical and devastating observation about sacred language. Words like "God," "Holy Spirit," "Christ," "sin," and "salvation" were no longer living words, words that carried a commonly understood meaning like "car," "tree," and "house." Most of these thinkers, including Tillich, didn't suggest the life force of the universe had expired. They said when people used the word, "God," they thought other people understood who and what they were referring to; however, that word now meant many different things to many different people.

No wonder there were 33,000 Christian denominations. No wonder religion was best left unremarked in polite conversation. No wonder most people, including myself, often failed to question whether their unusual experiences were genuinely transcendent or simply mental and emotional imagination: good for a momentary thrill, but not something upon which to build a life.

It took weeks of self-examination and conversations with Jess to come to terms with what this meant for my future. By Thanksgiving, I saw my upcoming role in a different light. As a priest, I was to utilize ordinary language to describe how the animating force of life engaged us each day—in theory and in reality. To do this, I had to locate that engagement in my own life, let go of any supernatural bullshit about it, notice how it changed me, and pass on to others what I learned.

I was captured by two understandings: sacred language was dead, and the job of a priest was to locate the human experience the language used to represent and make that experience understandable again. Experience was more valuable than belief: normal experience, experience at work and at home and at play, experience outside my religion and outside religion itself.

After all, "religion" was another sacred word that had lost its original meaning: to "re-bind" people to the ultimate source of their life. Instead, religion nearly always devolved to a set of beliefs and a code of behavior.

A week later, some of my beliefs collided with reality. And reality won.

GIVEN A COMPANION

Late one evening, I got a call from John Coats, a member of my original class. He'd also taken an intern year as an associate at St. Marks, Capitol Hill. It was the most progressive church in the area and was led by Jim Adams, a priest who had a reputation for telling the truth without sugarcoating it.

John's voice was low and urgent. "You're the fourth person I've called, and I'm hoping you can help."

My ego went to town. *Well, nice to be last on the list.*

"I mean," John said quickly, "I should have called you first, especially since we're both doing our field work at the Alexandria Hospital."

"Well, it's not like we're close friends."

"A nurse I know just phoned. Her patient just gave birth to twins, and one of them was stillborn. The mother is freaking out and insisting both babies get baptized so the one will go to heaven, and the other will survive."

How many things are wrong with this sentence?

"Baptized? Can we even do that?"

"Well, in an emergency, anyone can do a baptism ..."

"Yeah, but one of the kids is dead. Can we baptize a dead baby?"

"I don't know."

Now, my mind was churning. *Got to be careful here. The dean doesn't like either of us, and this could be just the excuse he needs to get rid of us.*

"I'll come with you, but we need to get permission to protect ourselves."

John paused a moment.

"I know Jack Beckwith. We can ask him."

Beckwith was our homiletics professor. He was distant and stuffy, but John seemed to trust him. Fifteen minutes later, John picked me up and we drove to Beckwith's traditional home: red brick with white trim, set in the verdant lushness of the seminary grounds. We knocked softly on his door. Professor Beckwith greeted us in his pajamas and didn't invite us in. We stood in the cold while John explained the situation and the nurse's request.

"Well," Beckwith said, "what's the problem?"

I intervened.

"Well, one of the babies didn't make it, and the unbaptized-not-going-to-heaven thing is outdated, and the baptism-will-keep-the-other-one-alive notion is terrible theology. Should we be doing this?"

"Hell, guys, the woman just lost one child and doesn't know if the other one's going to live. If she wants them baptized, you goddamn well go and do it!"

The hospital was half a mile from the seminary. Soon, I stood at a steel table in the cold morgue. The nurse handed the living baby to John, so tiny in his arms, and unwrapped the other body she'd taken from the refrigerator. I fought to keep my stomach under control as John calmly baptized the surviving baby and its little, gray twin. The mother was confined to bed and unable to attend. The nurse, relieved and grateful, put one child back in the refrigerator, next to two other tiny packages, and took the other back to her mother.

We stood outside the hospital for a long time, shaken but proud of what we'd done. It was the start a deep and lasting friendship. We soon discovered we had a lot in common. We were convinced the Death of God theologians were right: sacred language had lost its meaning. Radical truthfulness was required for people to let go of the beliefs that separated them from the daily experience of God. And when it came to ministering to others, theological concepts took distant second place to pastoral care.

GIVEN AN EXPERIENCE

In early March 1973, I lay in bed, anxious and unaware of why. I worked my way through the list of likely culprits: final seminary exams, securing a job in California, and working for a bishop I didn't know and about whom I'd only heard strange rumors.

I was confident about the exams. I was either first or second in my class and the new test format—three situational questions, each to be answered over a 48-hour period, demonstrating knowledge and application of everything we'd learned—played to my skill (analysis and writing) and avoided my weakness (memorizing facts and dates). John Coats already had a job in his diocese of Texas where there were plenty of openings. There were only three available posts in my diocese. In a month's time, I was scheduled to fly home for interviews and to meet Kilmer Myers, who had replaced James Pike.

I'd read Myers' book, *Light the Dark Streets*, and although it said a lot about his orientation to social ministry, it had little to say about his reputation of being a mystic. Mysticism: that word gnawed at me. For years, I'd dismissed mystical experience with Rudolph Bultmann's words: "The problem with mysticism is that it begins in mist and ends in schism." Anything mystical smacked of California woo-woo, of which I'd had my fill in the sixties.

Months earlier, my cousin, Prentice Kinser—we met Prentice and MaryAnn in Charlottesville when we first moved to Virginia—visited us in Alexandria to deliver the news he'd been "born again." He now spoke in tongues and wanted to talk because "I know you'll understand." I didn't, of course, and my ignorance chipped away at my confidence about being ordained.

In my last semester of seminary, I enrolled in a class on prayer. Ironically, it was the only class on the subject that had been offered during my years at VTS. It was led by Sid Saunders, the seminary chaplain who had stood by my side when Dean Woods had pushed for my expulsion. The class revealed how little I'd developed that side of my spirituality. I'd long ago given up my childhood's magical thinking about a supernatural being who attended to my requests if I made them in the right way. Other than having an occasional eruption of deep feeling, like swaying in the tree, sensing a call to the priesthood, and feeling a connection during the Eucharist, I didn't have a "prayer life."

That week, Sid assigned Kazantzakis' book, *St. Francis*. One night, I stayed up late to finish it. It uncovered a well of longing I'd first felt weeks before when I read a BBC interview with Carl Jung. He had said, "I don't need to believe in God, I know." He took a lot of heat for that statement, but for me, it opened a floodgate of feeling. And Francis' experience of God, that concept-shattering, undeniably physical sensation that struck him dumb and changed him for good, was so different from the occasionally moving, but largely intellectual devotion I often felt.

I didn't know how to get that experience, so I went to bed and just lay there, awake, wanting it to happen. The sound came first: a low drone, increasing in volume and pitch, like a swarm of bees rising from a hive. My chest imploded and exploded at the same time. I rose up and out of myself and dissolved into a cloud. I hovered over the four-poster bed where Jeanne and I lay. I flooded the corners of the room. I flowed into the hallway, billowed downstairs to the living room, and spilled out onto the street. As I got larger and diffuse, I also became smaller and concentrated. I didn't disappear; I distilled. I reduced to an essence, a central core, that was me and no one else. And yet I was also something much larger.

The drone increased to roar. The expansion and contraction pulled me further apart. Fear forced me out of bed. I walked around our apartment until the sensations eased. Finally, I went back to bed and slept soundly, but only for a couple of hours. At three-fifteen sharp, I woke up, really woke up: ears and eyes open, feeling again the imploding and exploding sensations, but this time I was able to contain them. I held them steady in that small, still place that felt most like me.

I got out of bed again, this time to retain the sensations. I walked to my study and sat cross-legged in front of the small altar I'd constructed for morning devotions. I made a deal with God. I'd give Him two hours each morning, and He could do whatever He wanted with me. I'd manage my fear, and He could take me where He pleased.

It was less a grand bargain than a logical next step. This connection was an *experience*, something I could feel, and I wanted more of it. I recalled my disastrous few weeks in college as a member of Campus Crusade for Christ. I usually felt embarrassed at the memory. Now, I appreciated the yearning that led to it. During the hours I spent each morning, I didn't always go "Walking in the Spirit," but undoubtedly I *rested* in it.

For the next couple of months, I awoke early, sat, or knelt, or crossed my legs Lotus style, closed my eyes, and did my best to follow whatever seemed to be happening inside my body. Often, that exploding/imploding sensation returned. Some days I had "ecstatic" experiences like visions and speaking in tongues. Other days were filled with boredom. I spent a lot of time corralling my resistance and letting go of "having" to experience what had happened before.

Graduation approached, and I decided to tell Jess Trotter what had happened. He listened carefully for a long time. "Sounds like you're getting somewhere," he said. "Keep going, balance the experience with study and reflection, and trust what happens. Let it pull you forward. You'll find your way."

We embraced, and his arms felt a lot like Dad's.

GRACE

The remarkable twists and turns of my senior year put my fears to rest. As I drive back to California, I'm more at home in my skin than ever before.

I conclude my difficulties are not fate's attempts to thwart my dreams, nor are they punishment for my shortcomings. They are the stuff that shakes me loose from illusions such as: I'm on my own, I don't belong, and I must be or do something special to earn the right to take my next breath.

I'm ready to see what I can do in a world populated with complex people driven by a multitude of desires. And how to discriminate between the forces that drive us all.

Chapter 6

TAKEN OFF THE LEASH

Age 26-27
Life brings more to see than meets the eye
Experience demands a loosening of the grip
On conventional beliefs and roles

"LIKE ARROWS SHOOTING UP"

I graduated from seminary, returned to California, and took a job as an assistant minister at Christ Church in Los Altos. We moved into a duplex in nearby Cupertino and met Ed and Kay Kinney, whose front door stood opposite ours. Four days later, early in the morning, I drove south to the St. Francis Retreat Center in San Juan Batista. I was to attend the mandatory Deacons' Retreat for the diocese's recent graduates. There were 14 of us who'd completed their time at seminaries throughout the country.

I would meet Bishop Kilmer Myers, my new bishop, whose reputation as a mystic had been tainted with the words, "and also an alcoholic." At his election, James Pike was reported to have said, "You have no idea who you just chose." None of that mattered. After the last few months, I was ready to meet someone unconventional.

I arrived early and walked the grounds. The simplicity of monastic life tugged at my heart, and the tranquility of the retreat center touched something deep inside that had been growing over the past few months. In the refectory, I saw a Franciscan recruiting poster, a drawing of a bedraggled St. Francis, with the caption, "Want to be a nobody?"

At eight-thirty in the morning, I gathered with the other graduates outside the small chapel that stood at the center of St. Francis' U-shaped courtyard. We were surrounded by white stucco walls, red-tiled roofs, and wooden pergolas that provided relief from the bright summer sun. We'd just finished breakfast, and the conversation had been muted. The scarcity of jobs in our diocese was common knowledge, and the clergyman in charge of placement had warned me that some of the other graduates were resentful I was employed. As we introduced ourselves, I tried unsuccessfully to sense who was upset with me.

A bell rang, and we entered the small chapel which was as spare and simple as the courtyard: very Franciscan. A plain, wooden crucifix hung over the altar, and small sculptures, set in alcoves on the side walls, marked the Stations of the Cross. A moment later, Bishop Myers emerged from the sacristy, stood in front of the altar, and welcomed us to the retreat.

"We just have a few days together," he said, "and we need to make them count. I'm sure you have lots of questions about your immediate future. Jobs are tight right now, I know that many of you don't have work, and I'm sure that is worrisome."

He paused a moment, perhaps to see if he'd read the room correctly. I wanted to look at the other graduates to see their reactions, but I kept my eyes on Myers, who continued to speak.

"Those are valid concerns, but they all take second place to questions more vital to why you're being ordained. Questions like: Do I really know Christ? Do I feel His presence? Do I know how to find him within and without? Over the next few days, those are the questions we need to ask, and answer."

I looked down. Recently I'd spent the majority of my time on things other than pondering those questions. During the past several weeks, I'd been consumed by the logistics of final exams, landing a job, and moving back across the country.

The bishop moved to the pulpit and began reading a meditation about parish ministry. Something about his words haunted my imagination. I understood the logic of what he said, but there was a disconcerting undercurrent to his thinking that unsettled me and undercut my confidence. After a while, I stopped listening. My body felt light, airy. I floated on his words. Here it was again, the sensation from four months ago that led to a deal with God: a bargain I'd recently not kept. Pressure built in my chest. It pushed in and out at the same time. My heartbeat slowed, slowed some more, and then it seemed to disappear.

I teared up, relieved and happy once again to have this sense of transcendence. But thoughts raced through my mind. How much of this sensation was genuinely "spiritual" and how much was self-delusion? This experience had led to a lot of discovery, but was it just about me instead of God? In the rush leading up to graduation, there were many mornings I'd skipped meditation. Were these physical sensations really important, or just something about which to feel special? And if they were so valuable, why had I stopped seeking them in favor of getting on with my life? I looked at the cross over the altar and thought: *St. Francis would have stuck with it.*

I looked at Bishop Myers. His mouth moved, but I heard only sound, not specific words. The rhythm of his voice aligned itself with the in and out movement of my chest: a bass line underneath melody. In that moment, I decided to tell him about the experience that several months ago had overtaken me. It *did* matter to me, even if I'd let it go for a while, and it felt right to tell him about it and seek his counsel.

The bishop finished his remarks, we celebrated communion, and after the service I asked when we could speak. He peered at me before responding.

"Oh, I think now's the time."

He led me to a small room behind the chapel that served as a sacristy and an office. He hung his stole on a wooden peg beside the single window, sat behind the desk, and pointed me to the wooden chair that faced him. He looked straight at me, parted his lips, but didn't speak. I wasn't used to people looking at me without saying anything. I felt small, insignificant, prey before a predator. His eyes sat deep in his skull, and they were surrounded by dark circles. Red veins clustered on his cheekbones. I remembered the gossip and felt guilty for thinking about it.

"When I listened to you in chapel …" I hesitated a moment. "When I sat there, I felt something I first experienced months ago."

He leaned in. "Describe it for me."

I took a breath and told him the whole story: the initial experience in bed and everything that had happened since. I left nothing out and told him I hadn't meditated recently. I talked for a long time, and at first, I felt lighter. As I forced myself to share more of the details, especially the experience of speaking in tongues and "seeing" things, relief turned into embarrassment. Was I disqualifying myself for the job I'd been given? Was all this just too … unprofessional?

When I finished talking, he remained silent, and as the silence grew, I felt the imploding/exploding sensation return and gather strength.

"That experience you're having right now, Roy, is that what you've been going through?"

I nodded, and his face softened.

"When it happens to me, I describe it as arrows shooting up from my body." And then he smiled.

My anxiety fell away, ice calving from a glacier. I wanted to embrace him, thank him, feel his arms around me. Instead, I sat there, tearing up. A moment later, fear arrived. I was exposed, naked. I was way too close to this man and whatever was happening between us. I had to pull back, gain some ground, put something between me and his probing eyes.

I cleared my throat and heard a business-like tone enter my voice. My words sounded strange, and they had a life of their own as they poured out. "Well, obviously, coming to grips with this experience is important for my development as a priest."

I stammered but pressed on. "In the past, when I've needed to learn new skills, I've made good use of consultants. Perhaps you could recommend someone who could help me integrate these experiences into my curacy at Christ Church, Los Altos."

The bishop's face clouded over, and he spoke slowly, with undisguised contempt. "You speak too lightly of important matters!" He took a breath and continued. "We do have 'consultants' like that. We call them spiritual directors."

I wanted to disappear. What an idiot I'd been. I had blown it like I always blew it: too eager, too pushy. I had my chance, and I fucked it up.

"Sorry."

He ignored my apology, waited a moment, and smiled again. "I'd be happy to be your spiritual director; please, call me Kim."

"GOD HAS NO VOICE"

Two weeks later, I drove north on Highway 280, heading for the bishop's houseboat on the bay below Sausilito. I drove past familiar sights: Stanford University and the linear accelerator, Half Moon Bay, and the Sunset district of San Francisco. I crossed the Golden Gate Bridge, made a sharp right, and descended into the artsy haven of Sausalito, where Alan Watts, one of my heroes, had once lived. I found the marina where Kim moored his boat, walked out to the slip, and stepped into the cockpit.

After standing a while in front of the steps that led down to his cabin door, I summoned the courage to knock. No answer. I knocked again. The same. A third time, and I heard a muffled reply that I hoped was, "Come in." I opened the door and walked into semi-darkness. Kim's bed was right in front of me, and he sat on its edge, in his pajamas, bare feet on the cold, wooden floor, a stunned look on his face.

I didn't know what to say, so I kept my mouth shut.

After what felt like a very long time, Kim returned from wherever in his mind he had gone. He seemed surprised by what he'd discovered. He said, "God has no voice!"

I did my best to maintain a straight face.

"Do you see what that means?" he demanded.

"Well," I tried to think. "I guess He has to communicate with us in ways other than words."

"Yes! Exactly right!"

That was the start of a two-hour conversation that wandered through territory as varied as the lives of St. Francis, Pope John XXIII, and the Italian monk, Carlo Carretto. Kim recounted his visit to a local Native American tribe who had invited him to a week-long sacred ceremony during which no one uttered a word. He summed up the experience by saying, "The silence was too eloquent for speech."

I didn't know what to say to that.

I did ask one question before I left. "What should I do before I see you again?"

"Every morning for a month, listen to Mozart for one hour. Then, come to Grace Cathedral and tell me what happened."

A DOG LET LOOSE IN THE PARK

I didn't own any Mozart, so I spent each morning listening to Handel's "Water Music." The inward and outward pressure often returned, but some of the reading Kim had mentioned—Caretto, Thomas Merton, and John of the Cross—warned me off feelings and sensations and encouraged sitting in silence. I didn't sense anything special happening, but I found a growing interest in other spiritual paths: Zen Buddhism, Hindu Yoga, Native American storytelling, and dream interpretation. I plunged myself into my work at Christ Church, Los Altos. I gathered groups of young adults to lead youth activities and Sunday School. I engaged them in T-group-like sessions, meditative exercise, and a class in "Christian Yoga."

One Sunday morning after church, a young man introduced himself as a protege of Episcopalian priest and Jungian analyst, Jack Sanford.

"I'm Hal Perry, and Jack wanted me to meet you."

I'd heard of Sanford, read one of his books on understanding dreams, but I didn't know him and I was sure he'd never heard of me.

I said, "I think he meant for you to meet Jerry Drino, over in San Jose." Jerry was known as the maverick priest in the diocese. Hal tilted his head and smiled. "No, I think he meant you." Within two weeks, I was consulting Hal about my dreams, and we became friends.

Harold Brumbaum, the Rector of Christ Church, my boss, and a close friend of Bishop Myers, once dryly remarked: "You're like a dog let loose in the park, peeing on every tree and bush you can find."

I took it as a compliment, even though that may not have been his intention.

HEARING FROM THE DEAD

My next spiritual direction conference with Kim Myers took place in his office at Grace Cathedral, a beautiful Gothic structure at the top of Nob Hill in San Francisco. His interest piqued when I told him that a month of classical music had brought memories of childhood.

"You know, Roy, when I read the lives of the saints, I find they often had their first mystical experiences very early in life. What do you remember?"

When I told him about the fir tree in Camarillo, he smiled. "I thought that might be the case. Anything else?"

At that moment, the memory of that forgotten Little League game returned. Kim hung on every detail. Then, he said, "Let's go to lunch. I've got someone for you to meet."

We walked downhill to the restaurant in the Fairmont Hotel. The hostess warmly greeted the bishop and said, "Canon Weaver is waiting for you at your usual table."

She escorted us to a corner booth where Kim introduced me to John Weaver, a longtime friend. He looked older than Kim, tall, energetic, with a florid face. He caught Kim up on his latest activity, including a trip to Krishnamurti's school in India and his latest conversation with Michael Murphy, the founder of Esalen. I was in fast company.

We talked theology, politics, and spiritual renewal. It was everything I wanted the church to care about. At Kim's urging, John told me about his work with the Futures Planning Council. The Council was a collection of task forces dedicated to exploring the relationship between Christianity and other fields of thought and practice: medicine, philosophy, science, education, politics, world religions, and New Age spirituality. Kim asked me to share my Little League experience. John listened with a glint in his eyes. Then, he asked me to represent him at a new task force he'd created to explore the relationship between Christianity and psychic phenomena.

Three days later, after an early Thursday dinner, I drove to the first meeting of the task force. I was curious, but cautious. The paranormal was weird, and the Episcopal Church didn't do weird. It claimed 14 U.S. Presidents as members, and it was the epitome of respectability. James Pike found little institutional support when, after his son's suicide in 1966, he held a televised seance with medium Arthur Ford, and a year later, published a book called, *The Other Side*, about his experiences with his dead son.

I didn't know what to think about the world of the paranormal, although the memory of Dad's death was always close at hand, and I did wonder about an afterlife. The task force meeting bored me tears, and when it ended, I headed for the door, determined to let Kim know this wasn't for me. I noticed one of the participants: an elderly woman who all evening hadn't said a word. She whispered to her companion, and he hurried after me.

"Mrs. Allingham would like to meet you," he said.

I tried to think of a way out and floated a few excuses about the late hour and a busy schedule, but he talked over my objections.

"You do know who she is, don't you?"

"I'm sorry. I've never heard of her."

"Well, next to Ena Twigg, Trixie Allingham is England's most famous medium."

I waited at the door while Mrs. Allingham toddled over to where we stood. "You must come to tea," she said. "Half-three on Monday will do." I drove home in a daze and spent the weekend wondering what to say to a woman who talks to dead people.

On Monday afternoon, I met her in the garden of the home they rented in Los Altos. She asked me to look at her scrapbook while she prepared the tea. The first page contained a press release for her book, *The Reluctant Medium*, published four years earlier. I looked at the author's picture. If it was her, it was either taken a long time ago or the past few years had been unkind.

The rest of the scrapbook contained clippings from a variety of local and national English newspapers. There were a few big stories; she'd persuaded a ghost to leave a famously haunted house he'd occupied since hanging himself after his wife's affair. The more recent articles were about her "sittings": personal sessions in which she reconnected grieving family members and friends to loved ones who had passed on.

Trixie returned to the garden carrying a tray that contained the makings of afternoon tea. She offered to "play Mum," and served us both, making sure I took three cookies that she referred to as "biscuits." She talked freely about her background: how her mother had been a medium, how she swore she'd never do the same until one night a man walked into the nursing home where she cared for a woman who suffered from cancer. "She won't die," the man declared in a strong, clear voice. "I was her husband whilst I was on earth." And then he vanished. Over the next few years, she was visited by an increasing number of people who had passed on. One day, when her deceased husband appeared, and announced his role as her guide, "I stopped resisting and accepted my gift."

She took a sip of tea, tilted her head, narrowed her eyes, and gazed to the right of where I sat. She leaned forward and said, "You didn't tell me your father had passed."

That got my attention, but I played it cool. "No, I didn't."

"Well, he's here, right over there." I looked to where she pointed, but all I saw was grass and weeds. She looked at the spot and appeared to listen. "Ah," she said. "He wants me to tell you he's sorry he left you so suddenly. He misses you, and he's proud of you."

I bit my lip and pressed a thumbnail into the palm of my hand. If this was really happening, it was extraordinary; if it was some sort of mind-reading or educated guesswork, it was a cruel hoax.

In a soft voice, Trixie said, "I know this is hard to believe. The first time is always difficult. That's why I always ask the spirits for proof that they're here. My guide always lets visitors know that, if they want to talk through me, they must prove they are here by providing information that only their loved ones know."

She listened a moment longer and said, "He says to tell you his first name starts with a "J."

"Yes, his name is Jess." I winced at my slip and wondered why, if this was on the level, she hadn't heard his full name.

Trixie said, "Never tell me; let me tell you. Otherwise, you won't believe this is real."

She was right: I didn't believe it, but God knows I wanted to. I wanted Dad to be there, to still be alive in some way, to know he was okay. But it was too much to hope for: too convenient, too comfortable. I feared being gullible.

Trixie broke into my thoughts. "To prove he's here, your father wants me to tell you he watched you last Wednesday evening when you hung that picture in the dining room and hit your thumb with the hammer."

Whoa.

I looked at my left thumbnail to see if the mark was large enough for her to have seen. It was, and my gut tightened in disappointment. I did the only thing I could think of: I started asking questions. I couldn't tell if Dad could "hear" me or whether Trixie mentally relayed my questions to him, but after each query, Trixie listened in silence and gave me "his" answers. Yes, he'd seen his father, mother, and his brother, Wes, who had died in the war and after whom I was named. He was fine, keeping busy with his assignments to help people who were still living. And would I please give his love to Jeanne. And he reminded me that he often gave her a gardenia from his favorite plant in the flower bed in the front yard of our family home.

This back-and-forth lasted over half an hour. Then, Trixie abruptly stopped talking. "That's it," she said, "he's gone."

"Do they always leave like that?" His sudden departure felt like a dismissal, and it hurt.

"Well, they don't have all day to talk to us, do they?" she said. "They're quite busy, you know. Everyone has a job to do, and it takes quite a bit of arranging for them to meet up with a guide and be available when someone on this side is ready to talk to them."

Comments like this made Trixie seem like the real deal. It was apparent when her personal and cultural biases crept into her reports of conversations with the Other Side. "Everyone has jobs to do" seemed more Protestant work ethic than eternal truth. To my question about whether people on the Other Side watched us all the time, from bathroom to bedroom, she displayed Victorian prudery as she confidently assured me those who were watching "turned their heads" when privacy required. And she was so convinced about her Anglicanism that she said of the dead, "eventually, they all come to Christ." Her obvious conditioning made everything else ring true.

Over the next 18 months, I spent many hours with Trixie. What finally eliminated my doubts was when Dad said Mom had taken his wedding ring and made it into two smaller rings, one for herself and one for my sister. I'd never known that. And, one day a "Father Joseph" showed up and made a prediction: in three months, I would be one of four candidates for the post of vicar at a brand-new Episcopal mission in South San Jose, and I would be chosen. And that's exactly what happened.

I couldn't fit that or anything else I experienced with Trixie into a theological category that made sense. And I tried. I even attempted to integrate into my work the mediumship skills she taught me. One day, soon after taking that new job, I talked with a woman whose husband had died. As Trixie had instructed, I closed my eyes and pictured a large square of black cloth: a background for whoever wished to appear. I saw a shadowy outline of a man, and I sensed his name began with the letter, "L." The woman confirmed his name had been "Larry." I tried to see and hear more from Larry, but nothing came. She said, "At least he's alive and well."

I smiled in reassurance, but my stomach churned. This was fine for Trixie, but not for me. I gave up trying to "make contact," as Trixie called it, and figured some unseen forces were mysteries beyond my comprehension.

THE EIGHT STAGES

A year later, Kim Myers asked John Thornton, the Rector of St. John's, Belvedere, to assume my spiritual direction. John introduced me to the practice of Contemplative Prayer, and it was the right thing at the right time. It gave me a framework to combine the practices I'd explored: my extended silences each morning, Zen sits, yoga, and even my mediumship work with Trixie.

He invited me to visit him overnight in Belvedere, a small city adjacent to the uber-wealthy community of Tiburon, across the bay from San Francisco. When I arrived at John's church, he told me he was in the process of separating from his wife, and we'd be spending the night at the home of a friend, Erik Erikson.

"*The* Erik Erikson?" I asked.

"That's the one."

I took a deep breath. I read Erikson's book, *Childhood and Society*, after a seminary professor casually mentioned it during a lecture. It was one of the early theories of normal human development, and it had planted a seed that spiritual development and psychosocial development were related.

When we knocked on the Erikson's door, his wife Joan answered. She invited us inside, and there he was: gnome-like, silver hair and beard, raised hands pressed together in a greeting of namaste to John.

The Eriksons immediately left for a holiday—the reason their house was available to us. That evening, I sat in Erik Erikson's chair, over which, framed on the wall, was a hand-written sketch of his eight stages of human development. I looked at his stairstep progression from Infancy to Late Adulthood, a journey from mistrust and shame to care and wisdom, and I felt my chest collapse and expand at the same time. And I realized something.

The human journey *is* sacred. My development as a human being *is* the odyssey to align with what I call, "God." The journey isn't about what happens after death. It's a quest for my real self, beyond and beneath the facade of personality. It's a pilgrimage to an alignment with the source of all existence. The sacred journey occurs in the ebb and flow of ordinary life.

HERE AND NOW

I race to explore every opportunity to experience the sacred. There's something effective in every path, there's the inevitable gobbledygook in terms of theory and belief, and there are things I simply can't explain.

My mother, for example, has a "reading" with Trixie. She wants to reconnect with Dad, and the session not only eases her grief, it somehow heals my relationship with her. Still, I don't feel completely comfortable with the various doctrines of life after death, whether Buddhist, Hindu, Sufi, or Christian. For me, what might or might not happen after death simply doesn't affect the decisions I make in the here and now. I'm unmoved by any promise of eternal reward or threat of eternal punishment. If there's any sort of afterlife, I'll find out about it when I get there.

Right now, my goal is to travel as far as I can along the paths that call to me. For better or for worse, the forces that shape my life, this life, here and now, have my full attention.

Chapter 7

BREAKTHROUGH AND BACKLASH

Age 28-34
Reality
A complex mix of darkness and light
That demands a stand and a thicker skin

THE SURVEY

I was 28 when elected the first full-time vicar at that brand-new Episcopal church in South San Jose. Aided by a no-interest down-payment loan from the diocese, Jeanne and I bought our first home in a new suburban development at the edge of a ten-acre field. We watched our house as it was constructed on a cul-de-sac nestled against the Santa Teresa Golf Course. Behind it, a low mountain range marked the furthest point south of the San Jose sprawl.

We moved into our new home in June 1975. During the next three years, we planted every bush and tree, laid yards of concrete, and built a large deck in the backyard. We hosted numerous gatherings of our new congregation, and I conducted Sunday services in the community rooms of local establishments: first in a small bank and later in Santa Teresa Hospital.

The diocese had secured two of the ten acres for a church

home. California real estate and construction were ridiculously expensive. The diocese purchased the first acre for $150,000, and the second was to be purchased by the church itself when it grew large enough to do so. The congregation planned to economize by moving an abandoned church—built in the late 1800s—from its original location in Gilroy, 20 miles south of the 10-acre field. That romantic plan gave the church its name: St. Stephen's in-the-Field.

Gilroy, California, is known for its annual Garlic Festival, and I drove there to see the building. What a disappointment. It was smaller than the chapel at Virginia Seminary, but it had the same Carpenter Gothic style. The pews for the congregation were fixed in a straight line, and the choir stalls separated the congregation from the altar, which was attached to the back wall, as far from the people as possible.

I immediately interviewed local architects and settled on a firm that appeared to understand the special requirements of modern ministry: the congregation gathered around and seated close to the altar, able to see each other as they worshipped. I took our new architect to Gilroy, and when he said it would cost nearly as much to move and retrofit the structure as to build something new, I canceled the plan. We kept the name, moved the church bell to the new site, and, in my garage workshop, I converted the old pews to contemplative prayer benches and created wall sconces that we sold to start a building fund.

Three years later, we started construction on a church home: a sanctuary that held 150 people in a semi-circle around the altar. The congregation sat in movable chairs outfitted with kneelers on the back. Large, round tables were stored in the sanctuary walls, and we used the building not only for worship, but for church suppers, youth activities, and neighborhood fairs. We had a single classroom building and two offices for which I built the furniture.

We grew slowly, and I thought the congregation would expand once we finished construction. Six months after we opened our doors, however, I noticed that none of our neighbors came to visit. I knew many of them well. We'd spent numerous holidays playing volleyball in the street and enjoying pot luck meals. They all knew this new church building housed the congregation of which I was in charge. They were all friends, but none of them checked out my church.

I conducted an informal survey with a dozen of my neighbors. "Why aren't you visiting my church?" seemed too direct, even accusatory. I opted for, "What is it you think I believe?" It took some digging to get to the truth, but the answers were variations on a theme.

You're a Christian, so obviously you believe every word in the Bible is literally true, Jesus is going to return soon and take you to Heaven while I go to Hell. I like you personally, Roy, but I can't buy all that. Frankly, I'm surprised you do.

My last conversation was with a neighbor I will call Elizabeth. She was a kind and lovely woman, whose husband was an associate pastor at a local "community Bible church." She assumed I agreed with her fundamentalist convictions and said it was nice to have at least one person on the block who knew the truth.

I steered the conversation toward social issues and opened the subject of the arms race. I said, "I'm concerned neither your church nor mine is doing very much about advocating a non-military solution to resolving conflict. With the proliferation of nuclear weapons, a new world war could have a devastating effect on civilization."

"Yes," she replied, "That would be terrible. But how wonderful it will be to see Jesus!"

That's when I knew extreme fundamentalism had hijacked my religion.

THE PYRAMID STONE

In February 1979, I took a three-month sabbatical. Building the new worship facility had taken a lot out of me. Once again, I had drifted away from my morning devotional routine and replaced it with non-stop activity to complete the building, start a school, and expand the congregation.

I arranged for three clergymen to look after the church in my absence. Jeanne, Josh—our 18-month-old son—and I left home and drove across the Golden Gate Bridge to the little town of Inverness. The secretary of the town's Episcopal Church had generously offered the use of a two-room guest cottage behind her home. I was determined to spend all 90 days immersing myself in the spiritual practices I'd accumulated: a combination of dream interpretation, contemplative prayer, I Ching divination, psychic conversation, and intensive journaling. All these practices were intended to take me deeper into myself, and I aimed to find God's presence in those depths.

Two months into sabbatical, the intensity of which was heightened by our cramped surroundings and my obsessive attention to instincts, intuitions, and imaginary conversations, Jeanne took Josh and drove to her parents. Her parting words were: "Do your thing, and I'll see you when you come home."

A week later, I woke up early one morning. I'd had a dream in which a pyramid appeared, accompanied by a man who told me this was the answer to my search. For an hour, I conversed with this man in my journal, but the exchange went nowhere. Discouraged, I closed the journal and started to make a cup of tea. As I poured boiling water into the pot, I heard the man speak as if he were standing right beside me.

"Walk into town!"

I'd spent weeks following such intuitions, so I left the guest house and walked down the road that led to the dozen buildings that formed the village of Inverness. As I approached the town, I again heard the voice in my head: "Stop! Look down and find the pyramid."

I looked to my left, at the shoulder of the road. No pyramid, just stones embedded in the dirt. A square-shaped rock caught my eye. I tried to pick it up, but it was stuck tight. I grabbed a stick, scraped around the stone's perimeter, and pulled it free. It was three inches tall, two inches square at its base, shaped like a pyramid.

I stared at the rock. Everything stilled. Above me, a bird cried as it flew. And in that moment, I *knew* the sacred and the secular were not two different realities, vying for my attention. There was one reality, a whole cloth, and "God" was the organizing force that bound the threads and held the weave. God was not external to my daily life, but fully present in everything that crossed my path.

Now the Death of God theology made even more sense than it had before. I reminded myself that my job as a priest was to find the sacred presence *in* my daily life and find a way to communicate this to my congregation.

This would prove easier to understand than to do.

THE SAVING OF SAN JOSE

A few weeks after I returned from sabbatical, and when I still struggled to express to my church what I'd learned, Bishop Myers asked me to represent the diocese at a meeting where an advance team for the Billy Graham Crusade were to meet with local clergy and civic leaders to explore the possibility of conducting a "revival" in the San Jose area.

There were three groups of people present: religious leaders, local politicians, and influential businessmen. As the dynamics of the meeting unfolded, I realized why these three groups had been invited. The Crusade staff's silky presentation overtly promised an increase in church attendance and covertly assured greater support for the politicians and businesses that sponsored the revival.

I was young, inexperienced, and bold. When it was my turn to speak, I shared the conversation I'd had with my neighbor, Elizabeth, about nuclear war and the Second Coming. I finished with a question: "What will the revival have to say about the political, commercial, and religious participation in a world that's facing such a threat?"

An awkward silence came over the group. Marvin Richter, the pastor of the largest Bible-based church in the area, Los Gatos Christian, tilted his chin down and raised his eyebrows. "I speak for 5,000 people who think this revival is long overdue. How many people do you represent?"

"Just myself," I said.

He grunted in response, and the leader of the Crusade staff called for a vote in which I was the lone, dissenting voice.

That moment confirmed the result of my neighborhood survey: that the cultural understanding of my religion had been compromised by the primitive perspective of Christianity developed in the early Nineteenth Century by Puritans who wanted to tame an uneducated and lawless Western United States. A century and a half later, the Death of God theologians noticed the result: "God" was up for grabs, and the loudest voices had won.

Over the airwaves and within what my friends derided as "big box churches," the fundamentalist understanding of Christianity had aligned itself with capitalism in some circles and patriotism in others. Its capture of sacred language failed to convey the wisdom accumulated by centuries of Christian development, and it obscured the reality of Christianity's painful forays into disastrous heresies, cruel crusades, and theocratic authoritarianism. This lack of understanding is exactly what my church history professor, John Woolverton, had warned me about.

I left the meeting, made my report to Bishop Myers, and during the next three months, I drafted a story called, *The Saving of San Jose*: a cautionary novel about the convergence of influence-seeking adherents, prosperity-seeking businessmen, and power-seeking politicians. I tried to get it published, and after it had been rejected, I paid a professional editor to read it. His feedback forced me to admit the manuscript, like Fundamentalism itself, was well-intentioned but overly simplistic.

The manuscript found its way into my sermons, and one of those sermons was heard by an influential member of the local chapter of the National Conference of Christians and Jews. I gave a presentation to the NCCJ about the impact of Fundamentalist theology on social policy, especially as it expressed itself in the Moral Majority movement spearheaded by Jerry Falwell. He advocated legislation, for instance, that criminalized the rental of a motel room to an unmarried couple.

Local television covered my lecture, and for a couple of months, I was hot stuff. I gave several lectures and appeared three times on Owen Spann's KGO Radio talk show.

Then, one Saturday morning, I opened my morning paper to the op-ed page, and I found six letters to the editor disparaging me by name and mentioning the church I served and where I lived. In their eyes, I wasn't a Christian. In fact, I was working for Satan and constituted a danger to right-thinking people in the San Francisco Bay Area.

The next day, conservative members of my church waved the page in my face and condemned the "negative attention you've drawn to our congregation." Only one of my clergy friends called in support; the rest maintained their distance. The message was clear; I was on my own, and I was petrified. I stopped appearing in public and concentrated on my work at St. Stephen's.

I couldn't decide if I was smart to withdraw from the fight, or simply spineless.

"GO KNOCK ON DOORS"

I was proud of what we were doing at St. Stephen's. It was theologically sound and enthusiastically accepted by many in the congregation, but the approach required the bishop's support. St. Stephen's depended on diocesan funding. We were a mission not a parish. I was a vicar, the bishop's representative, not an independent rector. I served at my bishop's pleasure, and all had been well when my bishop was Kim Myers. That was about to change.

Soon after my return from sabbatical, a group of us supported the formation of a new diocese. I had a good relationship with several progressive colleagues, especially after I quit warning the public about Jerry Falwell, and we wanted to separate ourselves from the conservative parishes in and around San Francisco.

Our work bore fruit, and a year later, in June 1980, we were central figures in the first Electing Convention of the new Diocese of El Camino Real. We were convinced ministry in contemporary California required a bishop with a modern skill set. At the convention, I nominated John Thornton, my spiritual director. He was eliminated in early voting as another man rose to the top. Shannon Mallory was already a suffragan (associate) bishop in the African country of Botswana, and his view of the church's role in society was far closer to the First Century than the Twentieth. Between votes, the conservative clergy and laity of California's Central Valley flocked to hear this man call for a return to "the basics of our faith."

Mallory easily won the election. A few months later, he paid his first visit to St. Stephen's in-the-Field. We talked for several hours, and I discovered we were pursuing the same goal: a robust, informed, passionate church that offered a perspective on human life and its possibilities that was different from the culture in which we lived. My approach, shaped by Trotter, Tillich, and the Death of God theology, was to help people verify their belief system and *experience* the difference between the forces that shaped their lives. His method, shaped by church life in Africa, was filled with evangelical fervor and constant attempts to convert members of tribal religions to primitive Christianity; he felt called to convert everyone to a Bible-based belief system and a strict code of behavior. I wanted to ground Christian life in contemporary experience, and he was convinced we needed to double-down on traditional language and customs.

I explained the rationale for my adult education program: its focus on biblical criticism, an informed reading of scripture, and the discovery of parallels with other spiritual paths. He preferred that I send forth my parishioners "two-by-two," knock on the doors of our neighbors, "bear witness to the Good News in Christ," and invite them to worship with us on Sundays. The more I talked about the growing interest of our congregation in contemplative prayer and its links with Zen Buddhism, the more he urged me to "get people praying to Jesus." And when I discussed the rapid growth of St. Stephen's School and its essential role in funding our facilities, he said something that let me know my days as a priest in his diocese were numbered.

"Schools shouldn't financially support churches," he declared.

"St. Stephen's School needs to serve our wider efforts to evangelize non-believers. I'm going to make the school part of the diocese. You need to grow the church so it can pay for itself."

Three months later, I preached my last sermon at St. Stephen's in-the-Field.

LEAVING CHURCH

I'm 34 years old when I walk away from an institution that nurtured me for two decades, but I don't walk away empty-handed. I carry scars from my encounters with Evangelistic Fundamentalism and mainline religion, and I have experiences that fit a nascent understanding of the sacred.

There appears to be a force within the forces that's somehow at work in the events of my daily life. The pyramid stone that sits on my desk reminds me I've experienced that force, and Tillich's definition of God as "The Ground of all Being" coincides with Jess Trotter's witness: "I've been to the bottom, and the bottom is firm."

More than ever, I feel called to be a priest, and more than ever, I'm convinced ministry is most effectively exercised in secular society. There is "firm ground" in *everything* that happens, no matter how difficult or dark.

I'm ready to discover what it means to be a priest outside the comfort and the constrictions of religious life.

PASSAGE III

In My Own Way

1981–2024 — Age 34–67

The title of Alan Watt's autobiography speaks to the necessity
of discerning the forces that drive me. How to trust myself
when I'm so adept at deception?
One step at a time, eyes open, maintaining hope.

Chapter 8

SENSING A WAY

Age 34–51
Liberation comes in many forms
And with it a desire to serve

I find a movement outside the church dedicated to telling the truth. Following that experience, I deepen my relationship with a man who becomes my mentor and years later, my tormentor. We decide to create a training program for the public that reflects our theological convictions. The result is a 20-year career that changes lives in unexpected ways, including my own.

THE TRUTH CAN PISS YOU OFF

"The problem with you motherfuckers is you don't know you're all assholes!"

On a crisp Saturday morning, I sat with 300 people in the ballroom of the San Jose Convention Center. Each of us had paid $600 for a ticket to the hottest show in the human potential universe: the est Training. Well, nearly everyone paid that amount. I traded on my status as a clergyman and was admitted for $50. After years of parish ministry, I believed this a privilege I deserved and considered myself clever for taking.

At precisely 9:00, the trainer strode to the front of the room and delivered his profane opening line. Finally. Something refreshingly different from the church culture I lived in and pressed the boundaries of for decades. This was a no-bullshit environment—reminiscent of the seminary T-groups, but harder on the ear. The overriding ethic was to tell the truth, especially about yourself and the "rackets" you employed to get by (like my sense of entitlement in paying only $50 for the training). Everything short of physical violence was permitted: profanity, insult, tears, and rage. And no subject was off the table. As the trainer put it, "In here, we deal with everything from the boardroom to the bedroom." It was straight talk on steroids.

I settled into my chair and felt at home.

The trainer's comments continued to spark outrage, but the upset was cleverly contained by two of the "ground rules" that governed participation in the workshop: "Don't talk unless called on by the trainer," and "When you are called on, wait for the microphone and speak into it so everyone in the room can hear." Those rules, rigidly enforced, prevented collective outburst and emotional escalation. They created an environment in which anything someone said could be highlighted, worked with, and utilized for self-awareness.

The training lasted a minimum of 77 hours: three Wednesday evenings surrounded two full weekends: four days that began at 9 AM and finished at 2 AM, unless the trainer decided to go longer. No one knew the time, because "Do not possess a timepiece in the training room" was also a ground rule. We had several trainers, men and women, all of whom were skilled at turning rage into revelation.

"You shouldn't speak to us that way!" one trainee said. Her voice rose in defiance.

"What way?"

"You know, using that language."

"What language?"

"You know what I'm talking about … the 'F' word and the 'A' word."

"You mean fuck and asshole?"

The woman's face turned red, and her voice got louder.

"Yes, and all the other words you use."

"Why not?"

A long pause.

"I don't like it."

"Where else in your life do you demand others stop saying things you don't like?"

And that question turned the conversation's focus from the trainer's language to the woman's life: the people whose behavior she disliked, the actions she took to change them, and the rage she often felt at her lack of control.

One man took a different tack, echoing the negative publicity that surrounded est and its founder, Werner Erhard.

"I heard Werner made 33 million dollars last year."

"Werner's always made a lot of money. What's your point?"

"Well, he used to be a used car salesman."

"Again, what's your point?"

"Well, this training is just a money-maker, isn't it?"

"You're afraid you're getting conned?"

"Well, yes."

"Who conned you before?"

A long interaction ensued: how he'd been ripped off by two business partners in whom he'd naively placed his trust, and how this betrayal had kept him from exercising his entrepreneurial skills and instincts.

By the end of the day, we'd heard from at least forty people, each of whom had been guided to share what they hoped to get from the training. They wept, they fumed, they screamed, and the trainer used everything to gradually develop an understanding among the participants that everyone had suffered, everyone had been hurt, everyone blamed others for why they didn't have what they wanted, and everyone used their pain to justify manipulating the people around them.

Our trainer summed up the first day's learning by expanding on his greeting. "You're all assholes, because you don't know your ass from a hole in the ground."

I felt my pride wanting to fight back, but I understood his point. Moreover, I envied his skill in gently and not-so-gently doing his job. I knew what he was talking about. I readily spotted asshole-ness—more easily in others than in myself—and how it expressed itself in darker forces like vanity, cruelty, and fanaticism.

The problem was I didn't know what to do with what I saw.

IT CAN ALSO SET YOU FREE

I expected the second day of est to be more of the same, and I looked forward to it. I entered the training room and obeyed the ground rule to "Take the centermost, frontmost seat." That put me in the left third of the room, second row, on the inside aisle. As I waited for the training to begin, I listened to the animated conversation around me. A few people were thrilled at the fireworks, many were appalled, and everyone had slept poorly. One woman's voice monopolized my attention. She sat immediately behind me, and if my mother had been a triplet instead of a twin, that woman could have been her second sister. Her vocabulary, her tone of voice, her sense of having been wronged—all of it echoed the constant correction and control I experienced in childhood at the hands of Mom and her mother who had lived with us. I felt irritated and afraid.

At what I assumed was nine o'clock sharp, the trainer strode to the front of the room, and the chatter stopped. He bounded onto the raised platform, turned around, and said, "Who'd like to share?"

The woman behind me grunted loudly. I glanced over my shoulder and saw her hand in the air. The trainer called her name, she stood, and when a member of the team sprinted from the back of the room and handed her a microphone, she tore into the trainer. "Thank you, young man," she said. "Quite frankly, after yesterday's ill-mannered display of vulgarity, I didn't think you'd have the courage to call on me."

I groaned along with crowd. The trainer's eyes widened, and he smiled. He glided across the platform, pounced onto the floor, stood directly in front of the woman, and said, "Tell me more."

"Well, you obviously weren't raised with any sense of decency or decorum, and your judgment of people is deplorable …"

And on she went, for at least ten minutes. She criticized, excoriated, and insulted nearly everyone in the room, especially the "crybabies" who had shared intimate details of their lives, details she labeled: "things best left unsaid in polite company." Whenever the trainer challenged the veracity of a comment or asked her to look at her own life more deeply, she didn't give an inch.

For the first few minutes, I sat with my head down, elbows on my knees, afraid I might throw up. A mental image of the immediate future took shape: she would explode, pieces of her flesh would stick to my neck and back, and I'd never feel clean again.

Time passed, she continued her rant, the trainer stayed calm, she didn't blow up, her flesh didn't fly all over me, and I started to relax. I turned my chair, leaned back, and settled in to watch what happened.

The trainer pressed her harder, and she gave as good as she got. Her voice got even more shrill, and finally she shouted, "If you keep this up, I'll never speak to you again!"

The trainer paused a moment and let her words hover in the room. Then, in a firm voice, he said:

"Lady, you are a cunt."

I stopped breathing, and it seemed everyone else did as well. That word … to a woman ….

"I beg your pardon!" Spit flew from her mouth and dribbled down her chin.

"Excuse me," he said, "that wasn't quite right."

"Well, I should say not."

"You, lady, are a motherfucking cunt."

The room was dead quiet. I felt lightheaded.

She cut loose. She howled, she swore, she raved. And the trainer never flinched. He occasionally raised his voice, but it was controlled, the way a preacher projects to the back of a church. Finally, she ran out of words. For a long moment, he let silence hang in the air. Then he lowered his voice and spoke with quiet deliberation.

"I bet you've treated every man in your life like this. I bet you're on your third marriage. I bet you have a son who won't even speak to you because, for his entire life, you treated him the way you treated me for the past half-hour."

I gazed from one face to the other. Hers was flushed and contorted, his was soft and relaxed. Suddenly, her jaw dropped, her eyes got large, and she teared up. The trainer backed off, and he waited.

"My God," she said. "You're right."

The trainer stayed silent, and her voice took on a tone of wonder.

"I am a cunt."

Another gasp from the crowd.

The trainer held up one finger, a reminder.

She smiled. "No, I'm a motherfucking cunt."

More silence. Then, she added, "You were wrong, though, about the details. I'm on my fourth marriage, and none of them have worked. And I have two sons, neither of whom will talk to me."

She broke into tears. I expected the trainer to reach out to her, to provide comfort and demonstrate care, like I'd done for years as a priest. But he just stood there, close enough to keep her company, far enough away to give her room to stand. She cried a while longer, collected herself, and wiped her face. I expected him to speak, to make a point, draw a lesson, but he stayed still.

She handed the wet tissues to the team member who perched at her side. The woman-who-sounded-like-my-mother-at-her-worst raised her eyes, and she looked 20 years younger. The wrinkles on her forehead and at the corners of her eyes had disappeared, and her face literally glowed like a figure in an icon. This woman's self-righteousness had cost her dearly, and, for the moment at least, she had let it go.

The Gospel of John came to mind: "You can know the truth, and the truth will set you free."

I wanted to be someone who told that liberating truth, that realistic honesty that can be frightening in the moment, but so relieving afterwards. I felt queasy about my prospects, but I longed to be that person.

THE HANDSHAKE

Ten days later, the morning after the final evening session of est, I had breakfast with my friend and colleague, Dr. Brad Brown. Brad was 18 years older and also an Episcopal priest. He left the parish ministry long before I did, earned a doctorate in psychology and, with his wife, Anne, ran the Institute for Family and Human Relations in nearby Los Gatos. Serendipity had brought us together following my discovery of the pyramid stone during my sabbatical. He worked as a volunteer priest at St. Stephen's for two years before I left, and together we enrolled in est.

We swapped stories and perceptions of the training. We analyzed the skills of the trainers, their objectivity and directness. We admired the structure of the training, the layout of the room, and the presence of a well-prepared team that supported participants during the exercises. We objected, however, to the underlying theology of the training. We agreed what est called "enlightenment" involved believing your will and God's will were united, that the greater good was served when you committed yourself without reservation to your own goals.

I was taken with the immediate results of est's confrontational techniques, but I wondered how easily the approach could drift into misuse and abuse. I knew a number of people who'd taken the training and adopted the aggressive, single-minded ethic of, "Give your word and keep it." I'd seen that maxim result in pushy, self-righteous behavior. It was no accident that, within a year of est's founding in 1971, the word "esthole" came into being.

Brad and I discussed ways to change the format and the training approach to reflect our own convictions about the nature of reality. We agreed on the need to reframe sacred language and locate God's activity in daily experience. We were convinced God was to be found in the normal events of life, and to experience the sacred involved facing the truth about those experiences. That required a way to embrace life with language that was fresh, direct, and respectful.

Brad said: "We should start our own training."

I reached across the table. "When?"

"Right now."

We shook hands, and I felt the calm in my chest give way to quiet excitement.

THE "LIFE" TRAINING

In September 1981, when we launched the Life Training Weekend, the culture seemed ready and willing to respond. Sixty-six people attended our first training, nearly all of whom were clients, parishioners, family members, and friends.

We adapted the layout and structure of the est Training: participants in horizontal rows in front of a raised platform on which we sat in tall deck chairs, flanked by two blackboards. We also altered est's approach. We replaced the "ground rules" with "disciplines" to create a self-chosen environment in which people could observe their behavior. We placed two blue and white signs in the front of the room that read, "Notice." We developed exercises that revealed to participants how their minds locked them into habitual ways of thinking and acting. We showed them how to utilize every event of their lives, especially the difficult ones, to discern how "Life" itself (our replacement word for "God") revealed their human limitations, exposed their duplicity, and called them to care for others. We owed this insight to Professor Edward Hobbs of the Graduate Theological Union in Berkeley, one of Brad's seminary professors.

I wanted to create a bumper sticker that read: "The Life Training: you're already in it. Why not learn about it?" We never adopted the bumper sticker, just as we rejected other marketing ideas provided by professionals who wanted us to succeed. Our marketing plan involved a Field of Dreams approach: Build it and they will come. And for a couple of years, that worked. People who completed that first training spread the word about what they'd been through, and within two months we'd expanded the program to three evenings and two long weekends. People traveled from different places to take the training, offered to organize trainings where they lived, and within a few years, we had established 22 Life Training Centers in four countries.

For nearly two decades, I had the time of my life. The transition from parish minister to human potential trainer and entrepreneur felt seamless. Brad and I offered a practical, spiritual orientation toward life, without the addition of sacred language. We helped many people face their disappointments, betrayals, and hardships in a way that empowered them to contribute to the good of everyone around them.

Ed Kinney, with whom Jeanne and I shared the duplex we rented when we returned from seminary, took one of our earliest trainings. He embraced the difficult reality that he and Kay couldn't conceive and decided he would find other children to care for. From that week forward, he spent Thursday nights at the Stanford Children's Hospital, volunteering his time in the cystic fibrosis ward.

A man I remember as Ezekiel attended our first "prison training" at Bastrop Federal Penitentiary in Texas. The next day, he showed me the exercise yard where he was allowed to spend a small amount of time each day. It measured fifteen feet by twenty, with high brick walls topped with razor wire. "I was given three consecutive life sentences for the murders I committed," he said. "I'll spend the rest of my life here, and, for the first time, I feel free." Within a week, he started assisting the prison psychologist in her work and doing what he could for his incarcerated brothers.

In the summer of 1990, when Nelson Mandela had been released from prison and campaigned for the presidency, I led the first Life Training in South Africa. I was invited to be a Peace Monitor on Soweto Day: traditionally a time of protest and violence that commemorated the 1974 massacre of schoolchildren by the South African army. At an information evening, after I presented the training and its possibilities, the Soweto School Principal urged everyone to attend. "We must learn to forgive our government for their years of brutality, so that, when Mandela is elected, we don't turn into our oppressors."

That woman understood the force of resentment and the work that people had to do to overcome it. The audience applauded, and she looked directly at me. I felt challenged and empowered.

Our approach didn't work for everyone. Some found the training too rigid, and life after the training—follow-up classes, workshops, and serving as part of the support team for future trainings—too demanding or inflexible. There were times, too many times, when we responded to someone's criticism or challenge about our methodology with a direction to "process" their concern. That meant, "Straighten out your thinking."

I remember a classmate from seminary, Bob Spencer, a deeply reflective man who attended our training and for a while was a leader in the Idaho community. After a few months, he resigned his position. When I phoned to find out what happened, he gave a blistering analysis of our leadership at the most recent annual conference and said, "You're a member of a cult."

We weren't a cult; people were free to come and go. But we were "cultish." We were awfully sure of ourselves and not open to other ways to help people respond to the events of their lives— and we rarely handled well any criticism that came our way.

Bob never spoke to me again.

GENUINE CHANGE

Over 20 years, I train thousands of people from around the world and witness thousands of life-changing moments. Next to the pyramid stone on my desk sits a Cross pen and pencil set, a seminary graduation gift from Jeanne. The black onyx base is inscribed with a verse from Ephesians central to my understanding of ministry: "To equip God's people for work in his service, to the building up of the body of Christ."

I'm now convinced all people belong to God, and anyone, anywhere, in any walk of life who wants to discover their true nature and follow where it leads is part of "the Body of Christ."

People can wake up, and they can change. It's a natural ability that yearns to be exercised. I've seen people abandon pretension, let go of ill will, and give themselves in service to others. It doesn't happen for everyone, but it happens enough to demonstrate the presence of a force that makes human transformation a possibility. There are also forces that compromise the ability to change, and the struggle between all these forces is subtle and deceptive.

I'm about to discover a painful irony: the more I help others find themselves, the more I lose track of who I am.

Chapter 9

GETTING IN THE WAY

Age 51–53
A painful reckoning
A necessary withdrawal

My two decades as co-founder of the Life Training Program is a critical part of my spiritual development. Thus far, it's the most fulfilling role of my life, but some unnoticed chickens come home to roost.

The ups and downs of my childhood—family conflicts, Dad's death, the struggle to fit in and stand out—generate a conflict of inner forces that first bring significant success and then sabotage it.

TWO HAMLETS

I was captivated by our sense of mission and seduced by our success. Over nearly two decades, our program grew, but we failed to develop an organization that reflected the transformational quality of our training. Brad and I disagreed on how to expand our program. I wanted us to slow our growth and take the time required to build a sustainable organization that could replicate itself. He trusted the pace of people offering to sponsor the training in their own communities, and he was convinced we should follow every lead.

I deferred to his opinion on this and other key decisions. In so doing, I ducked responsibility for our failures. I'd burned my bridges with the church and had no other way to earn a living. My financial needs blinded me to the slow and steadily growing struggle between us. It was years before I saw my part in the destructive dynamic of our relationship.

I remember an incident in the early nineties, before the start of a training in London. As Brad and I set up the front of the room, one of the team members looked at us and said, "Wow, the two of you training together. It's like watching Shakespeare with two Hamlets."

My belly tightened. Until that moment, I hadn't realized that during the past decade and a half, we'd fallen from partnership into competition, and I hadn't felt the fullness of the hurt and rage I'd buried inside. In nearly every component of our work, Brad demanded top billing, and I resented being the junior partner. We clashed over who invented what, how centers should operate, and who had the final say in any given decision. It was difficult to hold my love and respect for him alongside the rage and dis-respect that grew in my gut.

The psychic and spiritual load of our relationship—friend, mentor, business partner, father-figure—gradually became too heavy to bear.

GO ALONG TO GET ALONG

We made it through that London training, but along the way we clashed several times. On the flight home, I remembered the first time I knuckled under to what Brad wanted. In the fall of 1982, a year into our work, Brad and I sat at a balcony table in a Los Gatos restaurant. Baskets of colorful flowers adorned the wrought iron railing that overlooked a large courtyard onto which various upscale shops opened their doors. We often lunched there, and it epitomized the standard of living to which Brad was accustomed, and I aspired.

We discussed how to cope with the organizational demands of our rapidly expanding program. At that point, we had centers in San Jose and Houston and plans to open Atlanta, Knoxville, and London. We'd added a second weekend to the basic training, we'd created an "advanced course" called "All the World's a Stage," and Brad was on fire with ideas for more courses. We averaged 175 people per training, and we had money in the bank. We couldn't keep up with the logistical details of the business. We had office space to lease, teams to manage, supplies and travel to arrange, and trainers to train. We were overloaded.

We started a to-do list, and the crevice in Brad's forehead—what he called his "Grand Canyon of Concern"—deepened and turned crimson. He laid down his fork, looked at the center of the table, and spoke a little too loudly. "I don't want to administrate our program. I want to create the courses and train the trainers. I'm at a stage in my life where I'm going to do what I'm called to do."

This wasn't the start of a discussion; it was a line in the sand. He claimed for himself the activities we'd always done together, the work over which we had bonded and in which I'd played a smaller, but critical part. I didn't know what to say, and I waited for him to soften his demand. He stayed quiet, and his eyes bored into me.

I floated an idea. "Let's hire a CEO to manage the program, like Werner did with est. In his second year, right where we are in our own development, he hired an experienced administrator so he could focus on program development. We've got the money. Let's do that."

"No, we might need those funds for emergencies," he replied.

"Look, it's not that big a job; Tom manages the San Jose Center, and Ann takes care of Houston. They just need a little support."

My chest ached as my thoughts moved into high gear. *A "little support," my ass. And what about our plans for Atlanta, Knoxville, and freaking London? And all the other places that will come online as we grow? You're saying "we," but you mean "me."*

I gave it one last try. "Well, I too want to create courses and train trainers, just like we've been doing together."

I waited for him to say something, but he kept silent. He'd staked out the role he wanted, there wasn't anyone else at the table to pick up the slack, and I felt compelled to honor his seniority. He'd done so much for me; this was something I could do for him. I had time. I should be patient.

I heard my voice fill the void. "I'm willing to manage the organization." Being "willing" instead of "resistant" was a major virtue in our program. I relaxed into the inevitable and believed I'd made a rational choice. I would learn how to manage and build an organization to support our program.

"Great," Brad said. "Good for you. And, yes, of course, we'll work together on courses and with the trainers. Couldn't do it without you."

For a fleeting moment, I detected falseness in his voice, but I dismissed the thought as petty and unworthy of our mission. From then on, he wrote the courses, led the development of trainers, and I wrestled with the organization.

As the years went by, I kept telling myself I'd taken the noble path. My strategy was to be patient and someday it would be my turn to call the shots. Each time I "processed" my "mindtalk" about being left out of something I longed to do, I couldn't see that my decision to "wait my turn" was not a free choice, but a conditioned response. And my decision to ignore the hurt I felt further crippled the self-awareness I needed.

I completely underestimated my tolerance for pain and my capacity for self-deception.

THE BREAKING POINT

In September of 2000, I sat at the far corner of a large dining table in a restaurant near our Life Training Center in London. Twelve of us had gathered for a meal: Brad, me, and ten of our trainers. At this point in our twenty-year history, Brad and I struggled to be in the same room at the same time. He made more money than I did, and the program we co-founded was now referred to as "Brad's Work." It was a bitter pill, and I continued to swallow it in silence. The previous evening, we gave a joint lecture to our graduates in which we took turns presenting our individual perspective on two decades of working together. When we complimented each other, Brad said, "In all the years we worked together, you never said one bad word about me." My body twitched, and I'd spent that evening and next day unsuccessfully trying to figure out what bothered me about that statement.

At the restaurant, I wore a colorful shirt Jeanne had given me in seminary. In 1970, it was the height of fashion. Now, it was merely a bold statement. The shirt was too loud for Brad's taste, and he mocked it in front of the group. Some of our colleagues laughed along with him. Others looked at me with pity in their eyes. This was the latest in a series of similar incidents. In his attempts to be honest, Brad could go over the top. As usual, I tried to embrace his comment as "a learning experience." I acted humble and willing to take a joke, but inwardly, I seethed.

Later, at my hotel, I stayed awake for hours, reaching for the truth about what had happened. What I found was a twenty-year history of comparing myself to him. At first, our differences served my development. He was eighteen years older, well-traveled, steeped in psychological methodology, and he generously shared his experience, which included his mistakes as well as his successes.

After a few years, however, the comparison turned toxic. Freudians would have a field day with our father-son dynamic, and they'd be correct in their analysis. He couldn't treat me as an equal partner, and instead of standing up for myself, I used his weaknesses to compare myself favorably to him: he had affairs, I stayed faithful; he was unpredictable, I was reliable; he was dangerous, I was safe; he was harsh, I was considerate; he took credit, I applauded his genius. In my eyes, and I hoped in the eyes of others, I got to be the Good One.

At three in the morning, I discovered a painful reality that broke my heart: I'd lied to myself for a long time. I'd made excuses for his behavior instead of confronting him. I told myself it was for the sake of our program, but in truth it served my distorted self-interest. It was easier to blame him for our failures than to trust my own judgment, to defer to his instincts rather than risk following my own, to remain his partner rather than make my way in the world.

Twenty years of "working on myself," and I had failed to notice so fundamental a self-deception! I wanted to blame the program and our methodology, but I knew better. Noticing the mind's lies worked. I'd spent 20 years honing the practice, and I still got in my own way. I thought I'd been someone who let go of self-interest; in reality, I'd been a martyr. In "suffering for the greater good," I'd failed to make my unique contribution to my friend and our program. It was convenient to have Brad to blame, but feeling sorry for myself instead of facing my fears had cost me self-confidence, creativity, and my sense of being called.

I felt sick to my stomach and didn't fall asleep until the sun started to lighten the sky outside my hotel window. I felt anxious about what I was going to do, but I was determined. It had taken a lot of suffering to wake me up.

LEAVING OUR PROGRAM

I slept for a couple of hours and joined Brad for coffee in the kitchen of the London Center. I told him what I'd discovered about my co-dependency, my fear of being on my own, and how I played martyr instead of standing up for what I thought we should do. I looked him in the eye without embarrassment and told him the rest of what I'd come to say.

"I'll stay in my role until next fall, but when we get a new managing director on board, I'll take a year's sabbatical to start a doctoral program in the field of Transformative Learning and Change."

Brad's face lit up. "That's fantastic! It's perfect for you." He looked genuinely relieved, and his generosity kicked in. "But can you afford it? I remember how expensive my own PhD program was."

"I'll use my retirement savings, return to the Life Training Program in a year, stick to training, and see what else I can offer."

"And I'll raise money to help with your tuition."

His offer triggered the usual thoughts. *He wants to get rid of me. He's buying me off.*

I ignored the voices, thanked him for his support, and walked out of the kitchen.

THE POWER OF SELF-PITY

Over the next few months, as I withdraw from work, I find in my past multiple times in which self-pity has ruled my response to criticism or threat. I sense a strong drive toward kindness and decency, but I'm sobered by the pervasive impulse to feel sorry for myself.

The principal of that school in Soweto was right: We become what we resent. Self-pity is a debilitating force that generates martyrdom instead of self-awareness. At least, now I can smell it on myself, and I'm determined to stay clear of its stench.

I remember something C. S. Lewis reportedly said to his students: "God doesn't want us to suffer. He wants us to grow up."

I'm 54 years old, and I've still got some growing to do.

At least now I know it.

Chapter 10

FINDING MY WAY

Age 54–76
Grace will not be controlled
But it can be trusted

When I let go of wallowing in misery, other energies come forth: curiosity, courage, and willingness to explore.

It helps to have a living to earn. It makes my search expedient and realistic.

I'm on my own, and it feels just right.

THE SCHOOL

In August 2001, I started my year-long sabbatical and entered a doctoral program at the California Institute of Integral Studies (CIIS). The PhD program at CIIS focused on what was called Transformative Learning and Change. It was the study of how individuals, groups, societies, and cultures changed their self-understanding and behavior. The word, "transform," referred to a permanent, fundamental alteration in thought and behavior. Its study required familiarity with a lot of transformational disciplines, religious and non-religious, and original research culminating in a book-length dissertation.

The curriculum began with a week-long "intensive" held

at a retreat center in the redwoods in Northern California. I had enrolled in the residential program, and I wound up in a 28-person cohort, half of whom were former graduates who were there "to help the new people along." After a day filled with "going around the circle to make sure we hear from everyone," I decided this large a group, especially one with people who had already graduated, wasn't going to work for me. I shifted to a non-residential program and joined a 12-person cohort comprised entirely of new students. It was an eclectic group, including a Native American practitioner, a yoga teacher, a psychologist, a woman who had followed the Grateful Dead for a summer, and an advisor who played saxophone, was married to a popular jazz singer, and was known for his work on creativity.

I soon realized two decades of immersion in the Life Training Program had left me with a problem akin to that observed by the Death of God theologians. I was so used to my own esoteric language—"lifeshocks," "mindtalk," "verification"—it took weeks not only to "talk normal," but to appreciate the perceptions of reality held by my colleagues. I had a lot of "true believerism" to shed. I was used to people agreeing with me, not challenging what I thought or, worse, insulting me for it.

For whatever reason, one member of my cohort, a man I'll call Nick, took an immediate dislike to me. Two hours into our first meeting, he made a derogatory comment about something personal I had shared. At the next coffee break, I fumed about it to Matt, the yoga practitioner, whom everybody seemed to like. As had been my practice for decades, I wanted to confront Nick about his behavior and resolve the problem before it escalated. Matt suggested another approach.

"Don't take it personally."

"But what if it is personal?"

"Then," he smiled. "It's *especially* important not to take it personally."

Clearly, this was a new field of play. I decided to give his advice a try, and eventually Nick and I found our way past whatever had been the problem. I didn't feel entirely satisfied, but it did leave me free to get on with the work I was there to do instead of fighting every battle that presented itself.

"Being open" was a virtue at this university. The school avoided the restrictive boundaries of many PhD programs, and I flourished under its academic freedom. But I missed the linguistic rigor we'd brought to our Life Training work: for example, the discipline of noticing when we used the word "feel" followed by "like" or "that." Any statement that began with "I feel like …" or "I feel that …" wasn't a feeling; it was a belief, cloaked in emotion, masquerading as fact.

In contrast, the doctoral program advocated another kind of rigor. They called it "appreciative inquiry," and it required us to amplify the strengths in what people said and did, instead of pointing out the weaknesses. For me, this was difficult. I felt like (oops, I *believed*) this approach let a lot of fuzzy thinking slip by. After a year of effort, however, I had to admit it was exactly the way many people had helped me in the past: Mr. Orser, Roland Jones, Sid Sanders, Jess Trotter, Kim Myers, and John Thornton. It had given me room to stumble, fall, and get up again.

CIIS was a world that contained a multitude of books to understand, papers to write, and practices to explore. Being in my mid-fifties was an advantage. I'd already read a lot, been through a lot, and I knew exactly what I wanted to focus on. Over the years, there had consistently been one thing that changed everything for me.

And I wanted to know more about it.

THE RESEARCH

I wanted to focus my study on the profound experiences I'd had: the "sway" at the top of that tree in Camarillo, the swell of empathy that drove me to help my little brother build that kite; the call to be a priest; the imploding/exploding feeling in bed that night in seminary, and the experience of extended silence at the start of so many mornings.

The transformational literature called it by many names, but the most common and accessible term was mindfulness. I wanted to learn from people who had experienced it and who had developed practices to make it a part of their daily lives.

This desire took hold of me, and a few months into my doctoral program, I awoke early in the morning and opened my journal.

October 9, 2001

Anyone who has spent even two minutes in a mindful state and has been touched by its freedom, joy, clarity of mind and openness of heart, can appreciate its profound value for human life. I've got to be honest with myself about how incredibly important and incredibly difficult it is to sustain this state of mind.

When I started to identify what it was, I'd feel it happen and think, I've got it! Now, hold onto it … yes … that's it … you're doing it …. Then, hours, days, or weeks later, when I'd feel it again, I'd realize I'd been *asleep* for all those hours, days, and weeks: I'd been in a state of automatic pilot. I functioned just fine in my daily life, but I lacked that extraordinary awareness.

I thought about what I'd just written. Even though I now spent more time in a state of mindful awareness than ever before, I'd never be able to maintain it over long periods of time. I'd read about some people who had learned to do that, but I had to admit it didn't appear that I would become one of them. I changed my research goal: I no longer wanted to study how to maintain mindful awareness, but how to recognize a state of automatic pilot and then return to mindfulness as quickly as possible.

It took two years to prepare for my research project. I made a list of 250 books and articles to absorb, and I enrolled in eight workshops that looked promising. I envisioned a normal research project, quantitative in nature: a subject group, a control group, and a way to measure results. I attended a workshop at Esalen with Anna Wise, who claimed people could use EEG machines to train themselves to produce the theta waves present during states of mindfulness. When I proposed using this technology as a fundamental part of my research, my doctoral advisor referred me to an EEG expert Frank Echenhofer. Frank put me onto material that demonstrated this approach yielded unreliable results.

I then read about "qualitative" research: an approach more suited to transformative methodologies. One of the books on the subject made its case with an example. If I wanted to find out what it was like to be an impoverished child in a modern urban setting, I could read reams of quantitative studies that detailed poverty rates, scarcity of fresh food, inadequate housing, dead-end jobs, and absence of educational opportunities. And I still wouldn't know what life was like for that child. Or, I could read a qualitative study by a researcher who followed a poor child for six months and told the story of what he or she went through each day.

I decided to do qualitative research. I would pick a small group of people who were interested in increasing their experience of mindfulness. Together, we would pursue some sort of practice, honestly and accurately share our experiences, and I would draw conclusions about the effectiveness of the practice.

With this decision in hand, I started to execute my plan to read and attend workshops.

In late October 2001, I spent a week with Jack Kornfield and Stan Grof at a desert retreat center near California's Joshua Tree State Park. I knew Jack from his books on Buddhism and Stan by his research with Timothy Leary on the transformational properties of LSD. The retreat was a deep dive into Stan's Holotropic Breathwork (LSD was no longer legal) and Jack's focus on Vipassanā meditation. I found both practices interesting, but Vipassanā delivered more of the experience with which I was familiar.

Jack guided our group through the art of noticing and labeling thoughts as they occurred. This time-tested practice was developed by the Buddha. It required diligence and patience, but it worked. My years of contemplative prayer left me comfortable with long periods of silent withdrawal, and noticing my thinking was what I'd done for decades in the Life Training Program. Observing a belief as it popped into my head—a judgment, a threat, a prediction, an accusation—this prevented the thought from generating emotion and driving me to one action or another.

The retreat offered other experiences as well. For the first time, I experienced Buddhist Walking Meditation. I'd spent my adulthood running, jogging, and walking, but never had I restricted myself to a ten-foot distance and a pace that was so slow I could feel my entire foot as it made contact with and rolled over the ground. Neither had I ever been silent for an entire week. The depth of thought that provided! With no need to formulate what I would say, I had the energy and attention to uncover what I genuinely felt, believed, and desired.

I had the opportunity for a one-on-one conversation with Jack. I was eager to hear his input on my research project and on my next step to deepen what I'd learned on the retreat. His suggestion came with a significant downside, as I noted in my journal.

November 3, 2001

Spoke to Jack about my dissertation research. He said surprisingly little work had been done on mindfulness. He thought my angle about reality providing exactly the stimuli we need to wake up, to be mindful, was valuable. He leaned in as we talked.

When I asked for his recommendation as to next steps, he advised I join him for a month at Spirit Rock, his California retreat center. Then he smiled and said, "Actually, three months would be better."

I had a family to support, and Jack's suggestion was wholly impractical. The next day, when the retreat ended, another problem emerged. With a group of fellow participants, I walked to the bus stop to catch a ride to the airport. The bus was late. It was unusually hot, even for fall in the desert, and within 30 minutes, nearly everyone was irritable and filled with complaints. *An entire week of silence and meditation, and its impact wilts in the heat.* I knew from my own experience that, over time, daily meditation would work its way into my life. I also knew the process was long and fraught with self-deception. Surely, I thought, there must be something I can do to speed up the process: a practice I could use while at work and at home to wake me up when I'd fallen asleep *and* to help me return to the mindful state I experienced during meditation. A practice that didn't require me to separate myself from life in order to live my life with mindful awareness.

Two months passed, and I didn't find such a practice. Then something happened that supercharged my search. I received a call from the new managing director of the Life Training Program, who by then was having his own problems running the business.

"I've got some bad news," Scott said. "The program continues to suffer financially, and, after a brief uptick in enrollment, I've run into a lot of roadblocks. I'm calling to let you know what I just told Brad. Next August, when you return from sabbatical, I won't be able to pay your salaries."

I had no words.

"And I've got to be honest with you," he continued. "I'll do what I can to improve the situation, but when you come back, you're going to take the financial hit. Brad's got the advanced courses locked up, and his income is secure. All that's left for you are the Life Training Weekends and an occasional Focus Course. Unless enrollment into those trainings takes off, you won't make the income you need."

We signed off and promised to stay in touch. I sat down with Jeanne and broke the news. I wasn't sure how she'd react. We'd moved and built our dream home in the Sierra Nevada foothills. The Spotted Owl controversy had skyrocketed the cost of building materials, and we were financially underwater. Our daughter would soon enter college, and I had no idea what to do next to earn a living. Jeanne, whom once again I had underestimated, took my face in her hands and said, "I'm so glad it's come to this. I don't care what we do to make ends meet. We'll sell the house. I'll get a job. I just want to see you happy again."

My research now had an additional purpose: not only to return to mindful awareness, but also to earn a living. I pressed forward with my work. I traveled to Taos, New Mexico, and spent a week with Natalie Goldberg. She took a group of us through exercises designed to access what she called Wild Mind: a state of mindful awareness that could be achieved while writing without inhibition or self-censorship. With my doctoral advisor, I undertook an independent study on the relationship between mindful awareness and creativity. I spent a long weekend studying the Enneagram with Helen Palmer, one of the practitioners who used that Gurdjieffian symbol to understand human personality. I spent months practicing Jon Kabat-Zinn's "body scan" and the Vipassanā techniques I learned from Jack Kornfield.

By April 2003, I had learned enough to let go of these and similar practices as subjects for research. The overwhelming majority of mindfulness techniques were grounded in lengthy meditation and required withdrawal from daily life to escape the distraction and pressure that lulled people to sleep. I continued to search for a practice I could use to access a state of mindfulness *while* I worked and played. *That's* where the events imbued with sacred meaning occurred, and I wanted to engage them with the full beam of mindful awareness.

Then I reviewed an article by Charles Tart, a professor at the University of California, Davis. His book, *Waking Up*, had been influential in my thinking. When he discussed Gurdjieff's method of Self-Remembering, he included an observation that grabbed my attention. Gurdjieff noticed a mindful state occurred when you "split off" a small part of awareness to watch the rest of your mind deal with what life brought. Those words, *split off*, jumped out at me. I realized I could develop a practice that honored what I observed in the discovery of the Pyramid Stone, the processing of the Life Training, and what I'd learned from my time with John Thornton and Jack Kornfield. I used Gurdjieff's language (or perhaps it was Tart's language) to name the practice at the heart of my research proposal, titled: *Awake and Aware: Utilizing Split Attention to Link Mindful Awareness with Everyday Activities.*

I asked a small group of people to join me in this exploration. I completed the research in late 2003 and submitted my dissertation four months later. The results were encouraging.

As a group, we had learned how to return to mindful awareness by *making use* of what happened at work and at home,
especially when situations were difficult. We increased our
ability to *stay with* whatever occurred *while* we split off a small
part of attention to focus on something physical, something we
could feel in our bodies. We each discovered our go-to physical
sensation that worked best: feeling breath enter and exit the
body, sensing a foot on the floor, or touching middle finger to
thumb. Splitting our attention reduced or even eliminated the
mind's ability to pull us into judgment, anxiety, compulsion:
any sort of automatic reaction.

This technique wasn't a substitute for meditation. Each of
us had a regular contemplative practice of one sort or another.
What split attention did, however, was quickly return us to a
state of awareness at work, at home, wherever we were and
whatever we were doing. When we practiced splitting attention during moments that regularly occurred—for example,
answering the phone, responding to criticism, listening deeply
to the news—we consistently found ourselves able to think
more clearly, desire more deeply, and act more in alignment with
our core values. And an unexpected benefit occurred. The act
of "linking" split attention to a recurring moment—one of my
favorites was asking someone a question and then splitting my
attention while I listened to their answer—the event itself would
remind me to practice split attention. There was something
about the practice that was self-generating. My body and my
mind seemed to *enjoy* the state of mindful awareness. Perhaps
it even longed to return to it.

I was ready to test split attention in the real world.

THE CRUCIBLE

I graduated from CIIS in August 2004. By that time, I had started a career as a consultant and executive coach. One of my clients was an English firm that provided leadership training to multi-national businesses. Their methodology was derived from the Life Training Program, and Brad was their chief advisor. I didn't have the opportunity to bring split attention into that work, but I continued practicing it day-to-day. As the months went by, my skill increased, and in April 2009, I seized an opportunity to offer it to others. My longtime friend, Scott Roy, and I co-founded Whitten & Roy Partnership and combined our expertise: his in sales and mine in transformational technology.

Scott was a wonderful business partner: skilled, respectful, and creative. And we helped companies utilize split attention to execute a methodology we called Decision Intelligence Selling. We didn't use sacred language, and we didn't have to. A sense of purpose and commitment to personal values emerged naturally as salespeople and their leaders touched depths in themselves that generated compassion, responsibility, and commitment. And sales markedly increased.

In the beginning, we worked primarily with UK companies like British Telecom, Metro Safety, and Hitachi. Gradually, we found our greatest fulfillment in working with social enterprises that alleviated hunger, illness, and joblessness in the developing world. Split attention was an instant hit. Mark Campbell, Director of Sales for Hitachi, called it "the Jedi mind trick," and people used it to release what they referred to as "peak performance." I'd found a way to help people experience a sacred force embedded in their daily lives. It enabled them to quiet their minds on the spot when customers and colleagues turned up the heat. It generated perception and creativity when problems arose. It helped them find deep purpose in their work and the courage to switch jobs if purpose wasn't found.

I remember a man I'll call Brian. He worked as a sales rep for a large, multi-national company headquartered in London. He'd been given the account of an Asian telecom company with whom a deal had collapsed two years earlier. The company had refused to buy any more equipment until Brian's company repaired what they had already delivered.

"They were so pissed off," Brian said when we met with his group for an evaluation of the training we'd provided. "All they did during my sales visit was bitch about our service."

"What did *you* do?" Scott asked.

Brian smiled at the memory. "I split my attention and said, 'Tell me more.' It took a minute or so to kick in, but suddenly I was calm, thoughtful, and interested in their problem."

"And then …"

"My fear went away. I had zero need to defend our service, which in fact had been crap. I told them they were right to complain, and I explained why we had failed them: three critical managers had quit, and it was going to take a few months to right the ship."

One of his colleagues spoke up. "So, you walked away …"

"I used to get rattled and do that," Brian said. "And use our poor service as an excuse for why I couldn't develop a sale. But this time, I applied what we learned here. I helped them see our poor service was indeed costing them money. I even helped them calculate just how much. Then, I showed them it would cost even *more* to delay the upgrade of their equipment. That calculation was something they'd never considered."

"So the sale survived?" his colleague asked.

"The sale *doubled*," Brian said with a grin.

My work with WRP became the most fulfilling of my life. It

was now 2019, and I'd spent ten years in real ministry to the real world. I'd helped people find within themselves a place to stand and from which to respond to the needs of others. I planned on doing this for the rest of my life.

But, as Woody Allen once observed, "If you want to make God laugh, tell him your plans."

THE INSIGHT

In April 2019, I was surprised to feel a strong urge to retire from Whitten & Roy Partnership. By now, that sensation was familiar, and I trusted it. Unlike previous shifts in careers, I didn't have to escape something painful or reach for something promising. I didn't know what was next, but I trusted the impulse to find it.

It took 18 months to successfully withdraw from WRP and discover that what I most wanted to do was write. I had much to learn about sharing my experience in words, and in June 2021, I entered an MFA in Writing program at Pacific University.

Memoir seemed a natural fit, and reading other memoirists led me to Daniel Dennett's, *I've Been Thinking*. That took me to a YouTube video of his conversation with Richard Dawkins, Sam Harris, and Christopher Hitchens. The video was entitled, "The Four Horsemen of the New Atheism." I read books by each of them to see what they believed and why. I wanted to hear from solid thinkers, especially those who disagreed with me.

In *Outgrowing God*, Dawkins suggested time scale is critical for understanding evolution, and in *Darwin's Dangerous Idea*, Dennett elaborated on this observation. They convinced me of something I intuitively already knew: the beauty and complexity of evolution didn't require a supernatural creator. Something important suddenly made sense. I was aware of a sacred force within the events of my life. Now I could see this same force at work over billions of years, developing life itself, including the very gradual growth of single-celled organisms into human beings who could become mindfully aware.

For the Four Horsemen, this insight confirmed their atheism. For me, it confirmed the presence of the sacred in *everything* that existed.

AWAKE IN REAL TIME

I remember a conversation with Jess Trotter about relating theological concepts to everyday life. He shared more details about his own journey for sacred understanding, and he paused a moment as he looked out the window of his seminary office.

In a quiet voice, he said, "It takes such a long time to live out even a little bit of the truth."

Amen to that.

Sorting out the unseen forces that drive me has been a lengthy process, filled with hits and misses, breakdowns and break-throughs, suffering and joy. And finally, I know what I'm doing. I know how to listen to my mind, catch its falsehoods, and move into mindful awareness as I go about my daily life.

And that, as Robert Frost put it, has made all the difference.

THE ROAD AHEAD

A Future Worth Having

Age 77–Who Knows?

Daily, faithful choices
Determine not only my happiness
But the future others will inherit

It's been a long journey, but I've come to conclusions about the realities of my life and the responsibilities I bear toward them. I have convictions about God, darkness and evil, death and life, belief and faith. They are mine alone, I'm accountable for them, and I'm finally free of the need to convince others to agree with me.

Chapter 11

A PLACE TO STAND

What I'm convinced of
For now

There's a running joke originated by my children that makes an occasional appearance when I offer an opinion: "It's all about you, Dad."

It used to embarrass me. Now, I'm comfortable with taking myself seriously.

GOD BEYOND GOD

Following his son's suicide and three years of self-examination, my seminary professor, Jess Trotter, concluded something about the lowest point in his life: "The bottom is firm." After years of research, biologist Charles Darwin concluded that over a very long time, the adaptive drive of life itself produced the possibility of self-consciousness in human beings. I've watched thousands of people discover what it's like to be "awake and aware," and I've experienced it myself. Each time, I return to a profound sense of who I am and a deep desire to care for others, especially those who suffer.

It's not a heroic act, or even a particularly virtuous one. It's a natural process that leads me to an awe-inspiring conclusion:

embedded in the unseen forces that shape daily life, there is a *sacred* force, a drive toward wholeness and dignity that inexorably draws me closer to who I really am and the part I can play in the lives of people around me.

This is not a supernatural God that hears my prayers, gives me what I want, and protects me from what I don't. Neither is it an other-worldly being that blesses the worthy with wealth and success and abandons the undeserving to poverty and despair. This is not a God whose Son will soon return amid great turmoil and reward those who believe in Him and cast forever into outer darkness those who don't. This is not a God who, at our death welcomes us to Heaven or sends us to Hell.

As theologian Paul Tillich put it, this is a God beyond God, not a being among other beings, but the Ground of All Being: the ultimate reality that underlies and sustains all of existence. I believe "God" is the drive within life itself to *live*. It's the force that generates a huge number of diverse entities that require each other to thrive, even when their efforts to do so suffer the consequences of their own ignorance, blindness, and negligence. As Darwin observed: species that fail to adapt to reality fall by the wayside. When I think about the realities of climate change, political violence, polarization, dominance of the strong and enslavement of the weak, I don't doubt that life will survive; I do wonder how many human beings will be around to enjoy it if we don't align ourselves with the sacred force in which, as Tillich puts it, we live and move and have our being.

God is the process of life itself, and I neglect that process at my own peril. It is up to me to discern the difference between the force I experience when mindfully aware and the other forces that rule my life when I fail to pay attention to what I'm thinking.

AUTOMATIC PILOT

The failure to pay full attention to my mind and body, to what I think and feel, and to my connection with the sacred, is a painfully familiar state. I know the ease with which I can slip into a very functional sleep, a state of automaticity in which I can function as priest, trainer, consultant, husband, father, and friend, and remain blissfully unaware of who I really am, what I really want, and the role I can play in the world around me.

I don't sleepwalk through life because I choose to. I sleepwalk when I forget I have a choice. There are forces that prevent my remembering my ability to move into a state of mindful awareness. Fortunately, those forces are natural, not supernatural. For thousands of years, human beings created "gods" to explain and harness what they were unable to control: the rising of the sun, the raging of the sea, the vicissitudes of weather, and physical and psychological states they didn't understand.

I fall into a waking sleep each time I'm overtaken by unnoticed thoughts: erroneous interpretations of what happens to me and others, and the prejudices and predictions generated by these beliefs. My decades of self-pity were not the result of a demonic possession that required a supernatural fix. The cure involved a repeated humiliation that grew oppressive enough to drive my discovery of the cost and the payoff of feeling sorry for myself. The cure also required time spent in the silence of the here and now, until forgiveness of others and myself put me in touch with what the Hindus call my "original goodness."

In a similar way, the dark and destructive forces at work in culture, politics, religion, and economics are not supernatural either. They are the consequences of unnoticed fear, envy, and greed. And their hold on me dissipates in the face of events that are wondrous enough, or tragic enough, to shock me awake. Such events connect me with who I really am and what I most want to do. Events like these: looking into the eyes of my newborn children and knowing I'll give up my own life to keep them safe; working in countries in the Global South, and donating time, energy, and skill to relieve poverty and illness; and even beholding moments of profound violence—like the events at our Capitol on January 6th.

To my mind, the generosity, kindness, and self-sacrifice that naturally wells up in such moments is proof not only that destructive forces are self-generated, but that I can become attentive and skilled enough to respond in a life-giving way. Just as light has the power to dispel darkness, not the other way around, awareness, compassion, and gratitude dissolve fear and replace it with courage and care.

It's not that the sacred force chooses to bring me particular wonders and tragedies, although in retrospect it can look like that. It's that mindful awareness gives me the ability to embrace what happens and find the next step that is uniquely mine to take. The presence of the sacred is what allows me to take life seriously: my own life, the lives of people around me, and the life of the world in which I live.

And when I take life seriously, I take death seriously as well.

DEATH AND LIFE

When I think about dying, and I do that now more often than ever before, I think of three moments that inform and perplex me.

On December 6, 1996, I sat with my mother and her oncologist as he informed her that her pancreatic cancer was in an advanced stage. "How do we treat it?" she asked.

"What are your plans for Christmas?" he said.

"If I feel up to it, I'll spend it with Roy and his family."

"Why don't you do that," he replied. "Come see me after the holidays. We'll talk about a treatment plan."

I escorted Mom to the waiting room, told her I had another question for the doctor, and returned to his office. "Am I reading your signals correctly?" I asked. "That her condition is terminal, and she should just enjoy Christmas?"

"I don't think she'll make it to Christmas," he said. He gave me a small bottle of liquid morphine and instructed me to put a drop under her tongue whenever she felt pain. He looked me in the eye and said, "Whenever she feels *any* pain."

I got the message.

I walked Mom to the car, and I shared the doctor's prognosis. I knew she'd want to know. She teared up for a moment. Then, she set her jaw. "I need to get ready."

I noticed she winced as she leaned back in the car seat. I asked if she was in pain. She said she was, and I gave her a drop of morphine. "Well," she smiled, "that does work."

I drove to her apartment at Los Gatos Meadows, a retirement facility run by the Episcopal church. She calmly walked me through her home and identified the possessions she wanted given to certain family members. She also asked to cremate her body, disinter Dad from his twenty-seven-year-old grave, cremate his remains, and place their co-mingled ashes in the memorial garden at St. Andrew's Episcopal Church, our family's spiritual home.

She put her hands on my shoulders and said, "Don't let me suffer." Tears ran down my face as I agreed.

She squared her shoulders and said, "I'm ready to go be with your father."

A week after her death, I sat on the grass beside Dad's grave.

Mom had picked this spot because it was near a small oak tree. "You know how your father liked his trees," she'd said at the time. Now, the tree was fully grown. Even on a cool January day, I appreciated its shade.

Dad's skeleton lay next to me, under a white sheet, on top of a piece of plywood. The cemetery worker who had dug him up was on his hands and knees in the grave's surprisingly deep hole. I felt uneasy next to Dad's bones, sad I hadn't been with him when he died on the golf course, and determined to fulfill Mom's wishes.

Slowly, and with great care, the worker, whose name I never asked, collected every fragment that had broken off Dad's body. He lifted them like a precious offering and slid them under the shroud. I thought of Charon gracefully ferrying the newly dead across the river Styx. As I gazed at the shroud, peace rose in my chest, and my guilt and regret distilled into gratitude for the love and encouragement both Mom and Dad had given me.

The worker climbed out of Dad's grave. Up close, his weathered face reflected years of sifting gently through dirt in search of the last traces of people who had been loved. I extended my hand, he hesitated as if to say, "You do remember where this hand has been, don't you?" I did remember, and I wanted to feel that hand in mine.

I thanked him for his sensitivity and care. "Well," he said, "it's important."

Recently, one of our oldest friends, Kay Kinney, died. Half a century earlier, she and Ed shared that Cupertino duplex with us. Ed passed away a couple of years ago, and recently Kay wrote with the news she'd been diagnosed with Stage 4 cancer. It had spread to her vital organs, and she had chosen hospice over chemotherapy.

We drove to her home, where we had celebrated so many

New Year's Eves. We sat in her garden, near the fish pond Ed had spent so much time cultivating. Kay was calm, centered, at peace with her cancer-filled body. In the middle of our visit, we got to the subject of death.

Over the years, we'd had many conversations about sacred matters.

"How much longer are they giving you?" I asked.

"Probably a few weeks."

"What do you think will happen when you pass?"

She didn't hesitate. "Oh, I'll be with Ed again."

I want to believe Ed and Kay are reunited, that Mom and Dad are together, and, as Jeanne believes, she'll see her parents and brother when she dies. I also yearn to see my family and friends who have passed, even though, as my dear seminary colleague, John Coats, wryly observed, "Yes, but to hang out with them for *eternity*?"

Every major religion conceives some sort of afterlife. Even the Buddhists, who believe in reincarnation, are convinced of a transitional place, called the Bardo, where the newly dead either achieve liberation from the cycle of life and death or prepare themselves for their next incarnation.

If I had to bet—and despite the logic of Pascal's Wager, I don't think betting is required—I'd place my money on what Alan Watts wrote about how the Hindus view a human life: a wave that washes up on the beach for a short time and then recedes into the vast ocean of God from whence it came. At this point in my life, I think any conception of an afterlife in which I'm still conscious of being "Roy," is most likely a manifestation of my ego's fear of extinction, a fear I no longer have.

I'm not certain this is true, but I *am* certain no one else knows the truth either.

I often think about my year-and-a-half with Trixie Allingham, that lovely English medium. I can't figure out what she saw and communicated with during all those "sittings" I had with her. How she knew things I didn't: especially that Mom refashioned Dad's wedding ring and I would become the vicar at St. Stephen's in-the-Field. I think about Jung's concept of the collective unconscious which all human beings share and can access. Is this what Trixie was picking up on? I think about string theory in physics in which the dimensions of space and time are expanded and provide the possibility of multiple universes.

And I realize none of this makes a particle bit of difference to how I behave in the here and now. When Mom said, "I'm ready to go be with your Dad," I pledged myself to make that passage as easy as possible for her. When Kay said, "I'll be reunited with Ed," I didn't engage her in theological conversation. When people find in their beliefs the courage to face suffering and death, and when they don't take the True Believer path of forcing their opinions on others, I celebrate their courage and keep my mind open.

Writer and journalist G. K. Chesterton once said: "Angels can fly because they take themselves lightly."

I can take life seriously because I hold my beliefs lightly.

UNCOMMON SENSE

When my son, Josh, was five, I passed by his bedroom door and heard him shuffle through his toys on the floor of his closet. He mumbled, "Come on mind, don't trick me." I asked what he was doing, and he said, "I'm looking for G.I. Joe. My mind is telling me I'll never find him, but I know I will."

A children's book appeared in my imagination, and we "co-wrote" *I Think My Mind is Tricking Me.* We sold it at Life Training events, and a few teachers used it in their schools.

Months later, Josh received a packet of hand-written letters from a class of disabled children in Tennessee. The letter on top of the pile had a drawing of a stick figure walking in front of trees and houses. Underneath the picture, in scrawled block letters, there was a note for my son.

> Dear Joshua,
>
> My name is Joshua too. I'm twelve years old. One of my goals this year was to walk home by myself. I was always too afraid. My teacher read your book to us yesterday, and I walked home all by myself. I wasn't scared at all.
>
> I guess my mind was tricking me.
>
> Your friend, Joshua

I see what Jesus meant when he said: "Let the little children come to me; do not stop them; for it is to such as these that the kingdom of God belongs."

And I remember a comment from an older member of my church who had spent his working years on a farm. After sitting through a particularly long-winded sermon of mine on ethics, he said, "Doesn't it all come down to treating others as you want to be treated?"

Of course it does.

Attributed to Mark Twain is the compliment about someone's native good sense: "He had never been educated beyond his intelligence." I trust the education I've received *and* I trust common sense. Both have been essential to my search for the sacred. My intellectual curiosity demanded satisfaction, and it's helped to study the flow of ideas through time, the cul-de-sacs and rabbit holes into which thoughtful people can disappear, and the breakthroughs in understanding that light the way for others. My head is filled with books I've read, words I've written, and conversations I've had with people who dedicate themselves to sorting out the forces that drive them.

I'm compelled by something scholars agree was probably said by Jesus: "No good tree bears bad fruit, nor does a bad tree bear good fruit." I find it helpful to look at what people do, not necessarily what they say. Faith is action, not belief. When I see someone being kind, decent, and selfless, I trust their intentions. When I see demonstrations of greed, egoism, self-pity, and bullying, I put up my guard.

I also find it helpful to adopt practices that force me to bring mindful awareness to situations in which I easily become judgmental. California is an expensive place to live, and many people resort to begging on street corners and in front of businesses where I shop. A few months ago, I decided to give cash to anyone who asked for it, rather than succumb to my mind deciding who was worthy, who would spend it wisely, and who wasn't trying to con me. Recently, I handed money to a young man sitting on the curb in front of my local grocery store. He petted his dog and said, "Thank you." I heard myself say, "Thank *you* for the opportunity to give."

When I let myself do things like that, I feel light, happy, and free. I remember what the great cellist, Pablo Casals, then in his 90s, said when asked why he still practiced several hours a day: "I'm beginning to notice some improvement."

I remember a man named David Palmer, in whose home Jeanne and I lived when we first arrived in Virginia and waited for our apartment to become vacant. David was the Chief Engineer at the White House during the Kennedy and Johnson administrations. After he and his wife returned from vacation, and we had moved into our first apartment on Martha Custis Drive in Alexandria, Jeanne and I spent several Sunday afternoons on their patio. At one point, I made a cynical crack about voters, and David turned serious.

"There's one thing I've learned in my years at the White House," he said. "I have faith in the common sense of the average voter."

I didn't buy it then. But now I think he was right.

Chapter 12

A FUTURE WORTH HAVING

From: *Man and Superman* (1903) by George Bernard Shaw:
"This is the true joy in life, the being used for a purpose
recognized by yourself as a mighty one … the being a force
of Nature instead of a feverish, selfish little clod of ailments
and grievances, complaining that the world will not devote
itself to making you happy. "

Everything I do has an impact. It's all part of my calling.
Moreover, *all* men and women are called to be priests: to mediate
between heaven and earth, to feel and to follow that natural and
profound longing for the sacred, that hunger for home, that deep
desire to unite with life itself.

In my desire to serve the unseen forces, I have a lot of company.

THE COURAGE TO BE

In the spring of 1973, a month before seminary graduation, I sat
down for the last time with Jess Trotter. I talked about the pain
of my father's death, and he shared more of his grief over the
suicide of his son. He'd always been open about the value of the
therapy he'd received, and I told him how my own counseling
had helped me apply my theological studies to everyday life. He

confirmed our approach to authentic theology by citing the letter to the Romans in which Paul spoke of his human weakness: "For I do not do the good I want, but the evil I do not want is what I do."

Then he added something that got my attention: "Psychology can take you to the door of theology, but it can't take you through." Now, I see his point. The first decades of my search for the sacred were filled with psychological discovery. Roland Jones was right about my preaching the "Gospel of Sigmund Freud." But, I couldn't experience the sacred *without* the psychological awareness I acquired at Clinical Pastoral Education, the counseling I received from Bob Olson, and the collaboration with Brad Brown—including *all* the ups and downs of those years. James Baldwin wrote, "Not everything that is faced can be changed, but nothing can be changed until it's faced."

Before I could begin to sort out my deeper convictions, I had to notice when I was lying to myself. I had to accept my childhood sense of being special was both a delusion *and* a necessary pathway to theological understanding. That late-night meditative episode in seminary—when I distilled to an essential core *and* expanded into something diffuse and greater than myself—was an experience of both sides of this paradox.

I used to feel embarrassed when my kids would respond to my stories with, "It's all about you, Dad." Now I appreciate my willingness to risk being self-concerned. Clearly, *my* spiritual path requires exposing the delusions that cloud my understanding of who I am and who I'm not. And achieving that sort of clarity helps me appreciate the approach of transpersonal psychologists like Charles Tart and humanists like Greg Epstein.

I first read Thomas Merton's *Seeds of Contemplation* in seminary. He warned that it takes "heroic humility to be yourself and to be nobody but the man, or the artist, that God intended you to be." He cautioned that others will call your honesty "pride," and you can never be sure whether you are speaking from your "true self" or just defending your "false self." But he said this struggle helped you learn to "keep your balance" and "be yourself without getting tough about it."

I know what it's like to assert my false self against the false selves of others. I've done a lot of it. But I've also shared my true self with the true selves of others. I've learned, even when others criticize or oppose me, they're nearly always trying to find their own way forward, however blind, fearful, or stumbling they may appear. Just like I do.

I recognize why I was so drawn to that Franciscan recruiting poster at El Retiro Retreat Center. Something deep inside—beyond what I consciously realized at the time—knew how hard I was trying to be a "somebody": a priest, a trainer, a *someone* that would stand out, be respected, and, yes, do some good. It's taken years to appreciate Margaret Mead's advice: "Remember that you are completely unique, just like everyone else."

I've had many experiences that confirm my conviction that the desire to find the "door of theology" is a natural, universal longing. Jess Trotter reflected this reality when one day in class he said, "Everyone has a theology, whether they know it or not." In the fifth Century, Augustine wrote in *Confessions:* "Our hearts are restless until they rest in Thee."

The paths to this "resting" are many and varied. I think the light of the sacred comes to us through a prism. We may agree on its hue but debate its color; agree on the color but differ on its shade. When I quit arguing about my point of view and start listening carefully to the perspective of others, I appreciate the diversity of belief and non-belief in our world, and I'm better able to find that light shining in the darkness.

To do that requires a radical trust in myself and my perceptions of life: a trust that includes the expectation that I will once again deceive myself about something important. I rely on daily life to bring the challenges that call out the best in me, and that reliance generates a quiet and profound confidence: a certainty that I need not control the uncontrollable; a certainty that my right to exist is not something I have to earn, but a gift that can become a gift to the people I touch. Paul Tillich called this certainty, *The Courage to Be,* and he wrote a book about it.

I find that courage when I take *seriously* everything that happens—the wondrous and the catastrophic—and embrace it with as much mindful awareness as I can muster. Over time, this changes who I am and what I do with my money, my possessions, my skills, and my vote.

I'm finally at peace with what I've done and with what I've left undone.

But all that makes me even more aware of the struggles I have with the institution that nurtured me for so long.

THE USE AND ABUSE OF RELIGION

I've spent my life dealing with religion, in one form or another, especially my own. And I'm deeply conflicted about the role religion plays in our culture, our ethics, and the way we choose to govern ourselves.

On the one hand, religion in all its forms is *the* cultural institution that points to a sacred force at work in the world. Spiritual paths of all kinds, religious and secular, have empowered many people to recognize the darker forces within themselves, experience forgiveness for their failings, access their ability to transform their lives, and generate the courage to treat others with love.

On the other hand, spiritual paths are man-made, no matter how much divine inspiration they claim, and at one time or another, most of these paths have been used to justify war, slavery, conquest, genocide, and the physical and emotional control of others, especially the poor and the powerless. There is a *theological* reason why the laws of societal governance must be free from the dominance of any religion. In his essay, "Is Democracy a Good Thing?" C.S. Lewis wrote: "Mankind is so fallen that no man can be trusted with unchecked power over his fellows." Nothing gives a human being more unchecked power than the mantle of religious authority. The Constitution's separation of "church and state" recognizes the value of religious conviction *and* its temptation to impose a set of beliefs and behaviors; by not favoring one path over another, this separation fosters equality, respect, and decency.

I am deeply conflicted about religion in general and my own religion in particular. When someone asks if I'm a Christian, I don't have a simple answer. My reply—"I'm a follower of Jesus, and I suspect many who call themselves Christian wouldn't accept me as a member of their flock"—seems long-winded and defensive. Yet, that's the best answer I've got. When Alan Watts—who first introduced America to Eastern religions, and who co-founded the university where I studied—realized his theological views conflicted with Episcopal church doctrine, he resigned Holy Orders. Every time I consider doing the same, I remember two moments from my long life: my ordination, when Kim Myers took me by the shoulders and said, "Once a priest, always a priest"; and half a century ago, when Evangelical Fundamentalists shamed me in the *San Jose Mercury News*, and fear drove me out of the public square.

Now, however, I'm still a priest and no longer frozen in fear. I'm in for the long haul, and I want to find a way to use religion in my search for the sacred but not be used by it. I think Einstein pictured people like me when he wrote his essay, "Religion and Science." He described people who felt "the futility of human desires and aims" who stood in wonder at the order of nature and the capacity of human thought, and who possessed "a religious feeling which knows no dogma and no God conceived in man's image." He concludes that it's impossible for any church—or for that matter, any synagogue, temple, or mosque—to possess teachings based on this feeling.

This explains the struggle I feel when I go to church. I still find a sense of connection and inspiration in the liturgy, but I must constantly reinterpret or overlook many of the words it utilizes and the impact they appear to have on people around me. I've got enough education and experience to do this, but the effort required offsets the value I receive.

I don't take issue with people who practice their religion, unless they claim it requires them to impose their lifestyle on me. In good conscience, I cannot support the followers of movements like Christian Reconstruction, who believe the American government must be "Christianized" to pave the way for Jesus' return. I wish my church and other mainline forms of worship actively provided a robust alternative, but I don't see that happening on an effective scale. I don't go to church much anymore. I miss the Eucharist, I miss preaching, I miss officiating at baptisms, marriages, and funerals. I'm sad it's no longer a part of my life.

A WORLD WORTH PASSING ON

The January 6th insurrection presented a stark picture of where theological misunderstanding and misuse of sacred language can lead. It's remarkable anyone could watch the videos of those hours and conclude it was either a peaceful protest or the work of a few bad apples. It's remarkable that many people convicted of crimes on that day have been pardoned or had their sentences set aside. Even more remarkable is the attitude that somehow

"God" will pull us out of the cultural and political mess reflected on that day.

Recently, I discussed this with a pleasant, middle-aged man who scanned my groceries at the checkout counter of my local supermarket. After a minute or so of back-and-forth, during which I was unable to tell whether he approved of the riot or not, he put an end to the conversation. He pointed upward and said, "God will rescue us."

I agree with him. But I'm sure we have a different view of the timeline and results of this rescue. Those who believe in an imminent Second Coming—as did Jesus and Paul—often quote a line from Psalms and 2 Peter to justify why Christ hasn't yet returned: "With the Lord, a day is like a thousand years." I'm fine with that category of duration. I do think the sacred force will carry the day, just as it has in my own life. Life itself will survive global warming, political violence, and the degradation of our planet. I also think it's entirely possible that humanity—who generated the dark forces that created these problems—will suffer greatly in the process. As the innovative composer, Hector Berlioz once wrote, "Time is a great teacher, but unfortunately it kills its pupils."

I believe we must clean up our own messes rather than wait for a supernatural somebody to do it for us. I count on the interplay of education, common sense, and the darkness of reality to awaken us to our fundamental decency and the generative desire to create an inheritable world for our descendants. I'm convinced our collective awareness of the relationship between sacred understanding and political governance will determine the quality and the substance of the world we pass on to future generations.

I want to play my part in this next stage of humanity's evolution. To do that, I don't need to fight; I need to converse: to listen and to talk, intelligently, respectfully, and always with reference to experience of the sacred. In the first century, Rabbi Hillel put it briefly and well: "If I am not for myself, who will be for me? If I am only for myself, what am I? And if not now, when?"

FINDING GOD'S SIDE

During my four years in Virginia, I often visited the Lincoln Memorial. On the north side of its marble chamber is carved Lincoln's Second Inaugural Address. In the middle of that speech, Lincoln said: "Both [sides in the Civil War] read the same Bible and pray to the same God, and each invokes His aid against the other .... Our concern is not whether God is on our side; our greatest concern is to be on God's side."

I was 22 when I first read these words. I believed them, agreed with them, and only vaguely did I suspect how difficult it was to put them into action. The world is filled with people, religious, non-religious, spiritual, and secular, who appear convinced they know the right thing to do. I'm one of them. The question is: *how* do I know if what I'm doing is right? For decades, I mistook passionate opinion for truth, self-pity for humility, and success as proof of divine guidance.

What's the measure, the standard that determines if I'm on the side of *the* God instead of some deity I fashioned in my head to justify what I do? I think of Paul's letter to the Galatians in which he advises the early church to evaluate their relationship with God not by their beliefs, but by their behavior. He echoes Jesus' words about "good trees bear good fruit," and he asks that congregation to compare their conduct with the "fruits of the spirit": love, joy, peace, patience, kindness, goodness, faithfulness, gentleness, and self-control. That list is a bit quaint to the modern ear, but it's got legs—especially when you compare it to the behavior of many on January 6th and afterwards.

Many people claim to have an answer to the question, "How do I find God's side?" In my experience, their answers often devolve into a list of things to believe and ways to behave. I've done my share of doling out those lists, and I'm not proud of it. I'm humbled by my mind's ability to convince me its imaginings are true, and I've got a deep appreciation for Mark Twain's observation that I can be "educated beyond my own intelligence."

When I was younger, I *thought* I understood things—like marriage, fatherhood, patriotism—that I lacked the life experience to grasp. There's a great benefit to being older. I've learned to trust my own critical thinking about what I experience day-to-day: from the wonder of swaying-in-the-tree to the tragedy of January 6th. I'm aware how easy it is to fool myself, and how important it is to honor my doubts.

I'm still prone to arrogance, cynicism, and, of course, self-pity. I counter those forces as best I can by meeting the moments of my life with mindful awareness, feeling that old sway and stillness, and asking a few "right" questions:

What do I think about what's happening?

Which of my thoughts are factually true and which are beliefs?

When I'm mindfully aware, what do I most deeply want?

How will I act on this desire?

When I answer these questions *and* converse with people who pursue them in their own way, I feel informed, inspired, and filled with hope. Being mindful during these conversations is essential; it releases me from judgment and a need to convince others I'm right. And mindful awareness is magnetic; when I'm splitting my attention, I notice others also become more objective and respectful, confident in their own convictions and willing to let me have mine. This is firm ground, and I trust it.

Does everyone have to search for the sacred for things to

change? Not at all. Relatively few people participated in the struggles for equality and the right to vote; the rest of the people found themselves changing their minds. Commonly attributed to sociologist Margaret Mead is the saying, "Never doubt that a small group of thoughtful, committed citizens can change the world; indeed, it's the only thing that ever has."

I have no doubt when enough of us take seriously the search for the sacred in daily life, public opinion about the unseen force we call or don't call God will shed itself of superstition and fantasy, and common decency will prevail.

I want to play my part, however small, in bringing that about. And I'm confident I'm not alone.

Acknowledgments

In this book, I mention many of the people who have played a significant part in my search for the sacred—and how their wisdom, companionship, and humanity provided the challenges and the mentoring I needed to find my way. I won't mention them again here, and I hope I conveyed how helpful they were.

I could not have completed and published this memoir without the skill, generosity of spirit, counsel, and fellowship of several people who played a critical part in its production. I thank John Coats and Tom Parish for their advice and counsel; Catherine Parnell for her editorial skill and coaching; Jessica Gustafson for her feedback, proofreading eye, and management of my author website; Christa Johnson for her design of cover and layout; and Joel Block for his thoughtful guidance and support in creating the audio version. I thank the people who read early versions of the book and shared their experience, especially Josh Whitten and Briggy Kiddle.

I'm grateful for the many people who touched my life during my time as a parish priest, a principal in the Life Training Program—Brad Brown, David Templer the trainers, and the leaders of that program—and my years with Whitten & Roy Partnership—especially my business partner, Scott Roy, and our consultants and clients. I'm thankful for the support of The Rev. Mary Claugus and The Rt. Rev. Mary Gray-Reeves for the generous gift of their encouragement during my brief reacquaintance with the Episcopal Church. I also acknowledge with gratitude the faculty and students at Pacific University's MFA in Writing program, especially my principal advisor, Chris Abani, and the director of the program, Scott Korb.

And none of this would be happening without my family: Josh and Sara, Jessica and Dave, Amy, Olivia, Wesley, Hannah, and Chloe. And of course, my wife, Jeanne; we've had 60 years together, I'm greedy for more, and we'll take what we get with as much joy as possible.

BOOKS THAT HAVE HELPED

This is an "in case you're interested" list of books that have taken me places I found helpful to explore. Perhaps some of them will be of assistance to you as well.

- *A Confession* by Leo Tolstoy. First Warbler Classics Edition, 2024.

- *A Guide to Rational Living* by Albert Ellis. Prentice-Hall, 1961.

- *Abundance* by Ezra Klein and Derrek Thompson. Avid Reader Press, 2025.

- *After the Ecstasy, the Laundry* by Jack Kornfield. Bantam Books, 2000.

- *American Gospel: God, the Founding Fathers, and the Making of a Nation* by Jon Meacham. Random House, 2006.

- *Being Mortal* by Atul Gawande. Metropolitan Books, 2014.

- *Beyond Fundamentalism* by Reza Aslan. Random House, 2010.

- *Breaking the Spell: Religion as a Natural Phenomenon* by Daniel C. Dennett. Viking Adult, 2006.

- *Buddha* by Karen Armstrong. Viking Penguin, 2001.

- *Caught in the Pulpit: Leaving Belief Behind* by Daniel C. Dennett. Pitchstone Publishing, 2015.

- *Christian Wholeness: Spiritual Direction for Today* by Jess Trotter. Forward Movement, 2004.

- *Dark Night of the Soul* by St. John of the Cross. Image Books, 1959.

- *Darwin's Dangerous Idea: Evolution and the Meaning of Life* by Daniel C. Dennett. Simon & Schuster, 1995.

- *Doing the Truth* by James A. Pike. Doubleday, 1956.

- *Educated: A Memoir* by Tara Westover. Random House, 2018.

- *Falling Upward: A Spirituality for the Two Halves of Life* by Richard Rohr. Jossey-Bass, 2023.

- *God is Not Great: How Religion Poisons Everything* by Christopher Hitchens. Hachette Book Group, 2007.

- *God: A Human History* by Reza Aslan. Random House, 2017.

- *Good Without God* by Greg Epstein. Harper Collins, 2010.

- *Gurdjieff: Making a New World* by J.G. Bennett. Harper & Row, 1973.

- *I've Been Thinking* by Daniel C. Dennett. W.W. Norton & Company, 2023.

- *If This Be Heresy* by James A. Pike. Harper & Row, 1967.

- *In My Own Way: An Autobiography* by Alan Watts. New World Library, 2011.

- *Jesus and the Disinherited* by Howard Thurman. Beacon Press, 1996.

- *Letters and Papers from Prison* by Dietrich Bonhoeffer. Fortress Press, 2015.

- *Liberalism as a Way of Life* by Alexandre Lefebvre. Princeton University Press, 2024.

- *Lincoln in the Bardo* by George Saunders. Bloomsbury Publishing, 2017.

- *Living the Mindful Life* by Charles T. Tart. Shambhala, 1994.

- *Lost Christianity* by Jacob Needleman. Doubleday Books, 1980.

- *Memories, Dreams & Reflections* by C.G. Jung. Vintage, 1961.

- *Mere Christianity* by C.S. Lewis. Geoffrey Bles, 1952.

- *Misquoting Jesus: The Story Behind Who Changed the Bible and Why* by Bart D. Ehrman. Harper San Francisco, 2005.

- *Money and the Meaning of Life* by Jacob Needleman. Doubleday Currency, 1991.

- *One Taste: Daily Reflections on Integral Spirituality* by Ken Wilber. Shambhala, 2000.

- *Original Sinners: A New Interpretation of Genesis* by John Coats. Simon & Schuster, 2009.

- *Outgrowing God: A Beginner's Guide* by Richard Dawkins. Random House, 2019.

- *Saint Francis (A Fictionalized Biography)* by Nikos Kazantzakis. Simon & Schuster, 1962.

- *Santificum* by Chris Abani. Copper Canyon Press, 2013.

- *Seeds of Contemplation* by Thomas Merton. New Directions, 1949.

- *Self-Remembering* by Robert Earl Burton. Samuel Weiser, 1995.

- *Smoking the Bible* by Chris Abani. Copper Canyon Press, 2022.

- *Surprised by Joy* by C.S. Lewis. Houghton Mifflin Harcourt, 1956.

- *The Battle for God* by Karen Armstrong. Ballantine, 2000.

- *The Book of Form and Emptiness* by Ruth Ozeki. Penguin, 2021.

- *The Book: On the Taboo Against Knowing Who You Are* by Alan Watts. Vintage, 1972.

- *The Cost of Discipleship* by Dietrich Bonhoeffer. Macmillan, 1963.

- *The Courage to Be* by James Pike. Yale University Press, 1952.

- *The Creative Act: A Way of Being* by Rick Rubin. Penguin, 2023

- *The Death of Ivan Ilyich* by Leo Tolstoy. First Warbler Press Edition, 2023.

- *The Doors of Perception: Heaven and Hell* by Aldous Huxley. Harper Collins, 1984.

- *The Faith Between Us: A Jew and a Catholic Search for the Meaning of God* by Scott Korb and Peter Bebergal. Bloomsbury Publishing, 2008.

- *The Fifth Discipline* by Peter Senge. Currency, 1990.

- *The Fourth Way* by P.D. Ouspensky. Vintage, 1957.

- *The Gnostic Gospels* by Elaine Pagels. Random House, 1979.

- *The God Delusion* by Richard Dawkins. Mariner Books, 2008.

- *The Great Divorce* by C.S. Lewis. Macmillan, 1946.

- *The Inner Experience: Notes on Contemplation* by Thomas Merton. Harper Collins, 2012.

- *The Kingdom, the Power, and the Glory: American Evangelicals in an Age of Extremism* by Tim Alberta. Harper Collins, 2023.

- *The Mind & The Brain: Neuroplasticity and the Power of Mental Force* by Jeffrey M. Schwartz and Sharon Begley. Harper Collins, 2002.

- *The Monk and the Philosopher: East Meets West in a Father-Son Dialogue* by Jean-Francois Revel and Matthieu Ricard. Harper Thorsons, 1999.

- *The Practice of the Presence of God* by Brother Lawrence. Paraclete Press, 2010.

- *The Pursuit of Happiness: How Classical Writers on Virtue Inspired the Lives of the Founders* by Jeffrey Rosen. Simon & Schuster, 2024.

- *The Reluctant Medium* by Trixie Allingham. Regency Press, 1970.

- *The Sabbath* by Abraham Joshua Hechel (author) and Ilya Schor (illustrator). Farrar, Straus, and Giroux. 1951

- *The Second Mountain: The Quest for a Moral Life* by David Brooks. Random House, 2019.

- *The Seven Storey Mountain: A Journey of Faith and Transformation, Exploring Vulnerability, Forgiveness, and the Quest for Spiritual Fulfillment in the Midst of a Turbulent World* by Thomas Merton. New Directions, 1997.

- *The Soul of America: The Battle for Our Better Angels* by Jon Meacham. Random House, 2018.

- *The Tibetan Book of Living and Dying* by Sogyal Riponche, Patrick Gaffney, and Andrew Harvey. Harper Collins, 2002.

- *The True Believer* by Eric Hoffer. Harper and Brothers, 1951.

- *The Upswing: How America Came Together a Century Ago and How We Can Do it Again* by Robert D. Putnam, Shaylyn Romney Garrett, et al. Simon & Schuster, 2020.

- *Unearthing My Religion: Real Talk about Real Faith* by Mary Gray-Reeves. Church Publishing, 2013.

- *Waking Up: Overcoming the Obstacles to Human Potential* by Charles T. Tart. Shambala, 1987.

- *Walden* by Henry David Thoreau. Amazon Classics, 2017.

- *We the Fallen People: The Founders and the Future of American Democracy* by Robert Tracy McKenzie. IVP Academic, 2021.

- *You Are Accepted: In Conversation with Paul Tillich* by Ron Starbuck. Saint Julian Press, 2025.

- *Your Body Knows the Answer: Using Your Felt Sense to Solve Problems, Effect Change, and Liberate Creativity* by David I. Rome. Shambhala, 2014.

- *Your God is Too Small* by J.B. Phillips. Macmillan, 1961.

- *Zealot: The Life and Times of Jesus of Nazareth* by Reza Aslan. Random House, 2013.

About the Author

Roy Whitten has been a parish priest in the Episcopal Church, the co-founder of The Life Training Program and an executive coach and business consultant. In 2009, with his business partner, Scott Roy, he created Whitten & Roy Partnership, a sales consultancy that serves a wide range of socially conscious businesses.

He and his wife, Jeanne, have been married for over 50 years and have two children and four grandchildren. He earned a BA in Philosophy / Psychology from San Jose State College; an MDiv from Virginia Theological Seminary, a PhD from the California Institute of Integral Studies, and an MFA in Writing from Pacific University. He has written numerous professional articles and several books.

For more, please visit his website www.RoyWhitten.com and / or subscribe (for free) to his newsletter, "In My Own Way," at https://roywhitten.substack.com or scan the codes below.

WEBSITE:
SCAN TO
EXPLORE
MORE

SUBSTACK
NEWSLETTER:
SCAN TO STAY
CONNECTED

NOTES